05/13/07
198.87.98.185: I'm going to resist the urge to shoot. Be strong..
75.57.160.175: Is it hard to resisit?
198.87.98.185: If he could see me I never would, but on the inter
198.87.98.185: net we are so anonymous

05/16/07
68.35.52.162: Wafaa, I don't want to play. Diana
192.168.1.69: Diana you don't have to play you could protect me
192.168.1.69: by aiming the gun away.

05/16/07
213.40.103.203: wat did john an yoko lie in bed for?

05/17/07
128.36.197.38: so i told him...
128.36.197.38: "come closer to the gun"
128.36.197.38: when he responded,
208.120.102.67: he doesnt like that
208.120.102.67: said it in his youtube video
128.36.197.38: he became human to me

05/18/07
24.12.250.151: iraqis dont get a break
24.12.250.151: isn't that what this project is about??
87.127.36.214: its about many things

05/18/07
71.134.75.147: But I'm afraid most Americans will not get it...

05/18/07
69.3.220.149: this is how some people are experiencing life
69.3.220.149: who don't deserve this kind of treatment
24.16.235.85: ...what a great idea
69.3.220.149: and we, as americans, are so clueless what it's
69.3.220.149: like, that someone has to force himself
69.3.220.149: into that situation to demonstrate it for us

05/18/07
207.170.237.23: Internet = Point, Shoot, Click == Have fun!

05/18/07
24.17.243.50: why hasnt anyone stopped the man that started this

05/18/07
74.67.190.100: don't shoot him! he's a fucking human being!!

05/19/07
216.80.66.146: wafaa, i want to order you a pizza...
216.80.66.146: what do you want on it?
170.215.105.55: ahahahaha
70.49.252.14: I think I hit wafaa

05/19/07
83.184.50.114: This is bullshit, not art!
151.77.249.70: this is reality
203.213.7.133: ?
76.185.157.52: ?
84.220.151.144: thisi is art
151.33.61.182: cmon wafaa, where are you?
219.94.82.82: leave the poor guy alone
151.33.61.182: hey, shooting him is the whole point of all this,
219.94.82.82: no, the point is seeing whether people do it.

05/19/07
77.56.89.224: US kills confortably sitting on a sofa

05/19/07
24.99.34.128: come out and play little rabbit
86.11.142.253: i
172.202.85.50: where is he hiding
75.141.47.106: This is terrible. I applaud this mans courage.
70.53.185.32: Power is when we have every justification to kill
67.133.229.226: wow, an empty room. genius.

05/19/07
67.177.144.234: how on earth does he get any sleep?
160.129.6.245: and a poor guy getting shot by idiots
207.69.139.141: End the war NOW!!!
82.41.95.107: haha he is making his youtube video
82.41.95.107: he is behind plexy glass
65.29.60.88: ive always wanted to shoot an Iraqi

05/19/07
71.87.43.86: Who agrees to a one hour cease fire?
59.93.81.206: someone shoot him for stupidity?
83.160.37.253: not me. it's a duck range, with a big duck
216.15.126.76: .86: it only takes one to break the ceasefire
71.87.43.86: It can also only take one to make a stand
64.247.121.146: you're inspirational and i'm sorry if i hit you

05/19/07
69.118.231.53: If it were a real gun it might mean something,
69.118.231.53: but its just paintball

05/19/07
76.21.63.219: he signed up for this, how can it be wrong?
72.53.22.60: He's not even there. It's ok to fire the thing now
24.93.170.229: this gun needs to be made fully automatic.
72.53.22.60: he would go through about ten grand worth of paint
72.53.22.60: in a month

05/19/07
24.19.97.242: wafaa bilal... why do you hate america?
24.226.86.108: wats"Fapping"?
68.198.172.46: the U.S. (at least his school) supports this -_-
222.152.32.138: i tink he doesn't hate america, just showing u how
24.167.168.196: cant' stay in chat long before page changes
68.198.172.46: this shows how hateful americans are

05/19/07
24.6.2.33: I wish I didn't waste my bullet
218.218.134.158: I will not shoot. I want to be kind.

05/20/07
154.5.220.212: How the hell does this work?
24.19.97.242: he hides and you shoot at the walls
68.52.12.201: is this real
77.180.177.4: Yes.
71.246.248.234: who keeps clicking to the left?!?
68.198.172.46: Ok, I'm back. What did I miss?
77.180.177.4: The way war is waged these days, the people who
68.198.172.46: is he at the computer?
77.180.177.4: die, they have no more sense of the "reality"
77.180.177.4: of their acts than we have of this jerking image

05/20/07
66.92.11.131: does he chat with us? or just vblog?
68.198.172.46: I think he might go a little insane from this
67.184.125.190: He does actually chat with us, when he has time
67.184.125.190: He may be slightly overwhelmed right now
78.16.16.14: how do you control the gun?
67.184.125.190: use the left and right arrows to move the gun

WAFAA BILAL

WAFAA BILAL

Indulge Me

Bana Kattan

Museum of
Contemporary Art
Chicago

DelMonico Books • D.A.P.
New York

Ascendant Artist Series

The Museum of Contemporary Art Chicago's *Ascendant Artist* exhibitions present the work and ideas of lesser-known contemporary artists to our museum-going public. In 2018, we redesigned the *Ascendant Artist* publication series to focus on the unique factors that have led artists to this moment—the influences that drive their practice, the working methods that shape their artworks, and the evolving themes and subject matter of the works themselves—revealing the threads of their development and suggesting the promise of their future directions. These catalogues offer an accessible and affordable introduction to tomorrow's most relevant artists.

—

The opening and closing pages of this book feature selections from the online chat log accompanying Wafaa Bilal's 2007 performance *Domestic Tension*. As viewers visited Bilal's website for the performance, they could chat with him and one another as they waited for their chance to shoot.

6 Foreword
9 Acknowledgments

13 *"Cannibalism alone unites us": Wafaa Bilal's Imperatives of Consumption*
Bana Kattan

31 *Identifying the Edge of Reality: Wafaa Bilal and Lynn Hershman Leeson in Conversation*
Moderated by Bana Kattan

49 Images

94 A Note from the Curator

97 *Art, Life, and Living*
Wafaa Bilal

120 Biography and Exhibition History
124 Selected Bibliography
126 Exhibition Checklist
127 Exhibition Lenders and Sponsors
128 Contributors

Foreword

In 2007, Wafaa Bilal locked himself in a room in Chicago's FlatFile Gallery for thirty-one days, with a bed, a computer, an exercise bike, and a mounted automated paintball gun to keep him company. For twenty-four hours a day, seven days a week, he survived an all-out barrage of paintball fire as online viewers aimed their virtual sights on him. Since that historic performance, titled *Domestic Tension*, he has undertaken many more artistic projects that probe the limits of what is physically, technologically, and artistically possible. Moreover, he has continued to make work that calls his audience to account for their awareness (or lack thereof) of the difficult subjects with which he engages, and, crucially, to enter into a social contract with him and with each other.

Wafaa Bilal: Indulge Me, the Museum of Contemporary Art Chicago's newest entry in its *Ascendant Artist* exhibition series, is the first and largest survey of Bilal's far-reaching work, bringing together five projects made by the artist over a nearly twenty-year span. In that time, Bilal has gone so far as to surgically implant a camera into the back of his head and, for an entire year, capture the minute-by-minute snapshots of whatever was behind him; he has collaborated with scientists to encode a digital surrogate of an Assyrian lamassu sculpture into the DNA of a wheat seed; and, on the occasion of this exhibition, he has even started working beyond our planet's surface by launching a miniature golden bust of Saddam Hussein into Earth's lower orbit, where it will drift for a time before burning up upon reentry into the atmosphere. What these and other visionary works by Bilal reveal is an artist who is not only creating at the very edge of what is possible but living there—often by adopting and adapting methods and tools from nascent technologies, ranging from genetic engineering to miniaturized satellites. The MCA exhibition and this accompanying publication are critical documents of this daring artistic existence.

Curating such a complex and deeply engaging exhibition requires foresight, expertise, and rigor—qualities which are inherent to the MCA's Pamela Alper Associate Curator Bana Kattan. I'm grateful for her work on the exhibition and this publication, as well as for her close collaboration with the artist. Their partnership underscores an energetic exchange that is indicative of both Bilal's generosity and openness and Bana's creativity and intellectual acumen. As a curator, she truly embodies what it means to be a champion for revelatory art and artists. The exhibition is also a full circle moment for Bilal, whose career gained a first foothold in Chicago in 2007. I thank Bana as well for her help in facilitating his much-anticipated return.

Of course, this exhibition would not be possible—nor would the larger series of which it is a part—without the devotion of some of the MCA's closest philanthropic partners. Lead support for *Wafaa Bilal: Indulge Me* was provided by the Harris Family Foundation in memory of Bette and Neison Harris, the Zell Family Foundation, and Cari and Michael Sacks, while generous support was provided by Creative Capital Foundation, The Joyce Foundation, and the Margot and W. George Greig Ascendant Artist Fund. Their support of this exhibition and of series like *Ascendant Artist* enable the MCA to foster its relationships with an ever-growing contingent of vanguard artists who, like Bilal, are not only creating the future but finding the most interesting and engaging ways of getting us there.

For Bilal, that process has necessarily involved a few key strategies, namely: interactivity, participation, and collaboration. These inclusive practices form the core of his work, and across decades of art making they have materialized in myriad ways. They show up in his multidisciplinary engagement with scientists, technologists, and engineers, as well as other artists, who have each aided in the production of his inventive undertakings. They take shape through the critical interactions, both virtual and physical, between himself and his audience. These efforts have even, at times, come at the expense of his own body, which he has frequently made the vessel for this mode of interactive art—whether by putting himself in the line of fire, surgically altering his body, or making provocative political art that brings with it a cascade of protests and threats against him. Whatever the circumstance, Bilal has remained steadfast in his commitment to creating pathways for connection, because within that connection lies the future Bilal has spent his entire career pursuing with grace and integrity. It is a future where the divisions he sees drawn between *here* and *there*, or *myself* and *other*, are dissolved and a collective sense of humanity prevails.

Needless to say, the path Bilal is charting for us is not an easy one. It requires radical imagination and fervent empathy. It demands that we look at the conditions of our present existence and recognize the tremendous suffering in the world around us, including that in which we may take some part, even if indirectly. It asks that we open ourselves up to the pain of others. Yet, through his work, Bilal himself shows us that it is possible for radical transformation through genuine human connection to take root, and even flourish.

Madeleine Grynsztejn
Pritzker Director
Museum of Contemporary Art Chicago

Acknowledgments

I first met Wafaa Bilal on a bench in Washington Square Park in New York, almost ten years ago (Wafaa splits his studio time between this bench and a more traditional studio space at the Elizabeth Center for the Arts). Since that momentous day, I have had the opportunity to commission and exhibit his work in 2017 and again for this exhibition, *Wafaa Bilal: Indulge Me*, in 2025. Over the course of the intervening decade, I have often reflected on the prescience of Wafaa's practice and the novel connections his projects continue to forge as the world evolves. In fact, his work often seems to forecast the unanticipated applications and ethical issues that ultimately arise from new technology. Viewing Wafaa's work reminds us that we are constantly engaged in a connected and mutable world. His discernment of the limits and failures of our systems, power structures, and governments is both constructive and playful.

I want to thank Wafaa first for entrusting me with the task of framing his work for this survey, as well as for his brilliance, his extraordinary generosity, his humor, and his sense of perspective, which I believe puts him at the forefront of thinkers on the role of art in our uncertain, grief-bound world. Within this volume, he observes that for art to be effective, it must have a clarity of purpose, and it must build genuine human connection, "even in the face of injustice and oppression." There is no more succinct description of Wafaa's work and how he operates as an artist.

For their leadership and enthusiastic support of Wafaa's work through the exhibition, as well as their support of Wafaa's newly commissioned project, I want to thank Pritzker Director Madeleine Grynsztejn, Deputy Director and Chief of Curatorial Affairs Joey Orr, and Manilow Senior Curator Jamillah James. A special thanks is also due to Curatorial Associate Iris Colburn, whose critical work was instrumental in developing this exhibition.

This book's engaging and lively form has been made possible by the efforts of the brilliant publications team at the MCA, to whom I am endlessly grateful. Under the leadership of Director of Content Strategy Kelsey Campbell-Dollaghan and Associate Director of Editorial Tyler Laminack, I have been met with incredible thought partners through every stage of the development of this manuscript. The publication also owes a great deal to the creativity and resourcefulness of the Rights and Images team: Associate Director of Rights and Images Katie Levi and Coordinator of Rights and Images Gabrielle Banks. My gratitude for designer Larry Issa, whose quick thinking and skill is evident throughout these pages, is immense. I am also grateful for the assistance of our interns, Akaelah Flotho, Luke Immins, Marcelo Quesada, and Ricky Reyes, with a special thanks to Kamala GhaneaBassiri, whose research was invaluable to this publication. And thank you to the team at DelMonico Books for their unwavering support in helping us bring Wafaa Bilal's work to a broader audience.

Many more wonderful people lent their hands to this exhibition, and their efforts do not go unrecognized. Among the teams who made *Wafaa Bilal: Indulge Me* possible, I must recognize the Artistic Division, including the Collections and Exhibitions team, whose careful work brought some of Wafaa's most ephemeral and fleeting artworks into being within the galleries; the Learning team for their creativity in facilitating educational engagement around the exhibition; and the Interpretation team for their thoughtful shepherding of the exhibition's key ideas. I also thank the Development team for their tireless work and their excitement about this exhibition; and the Communications, Content, and Creative Division for their steadfast and thoughtful approach to bringing our collective work into the public eye. Finally, I have immense gratitude for the Operations Division, including Audience Experience, Retail Experience, Visitor and Event Experience, Accounting, People and Culture, and Building Operations, for their incredible flexibility and support across our many avenues of collaboration. I would also like to acknowledge Director of Production Paul Deuth, Director of Interpretation and In-Gallery Learning Jeremy Kreusch, and Video Production Manager Sam Clapp for the dynamic and comprehensive video that accompanies the exhibition: your care shines through your work on this project.

This publication represents years of research, discussion, and work on the part of Wafaa and many others. I thank Wafaa for his intensive collaboration and for his powerful essay, which makes a compelling argument for the role of the artist in society today, as well as the deeply personal and poignant reflections that accompany it. I also owe a debt of gratitude to the brilliant Lynn Hershman Leeson, who showed no hesitation in spending hours with myself and Wafaa engaged in fascinating and far-ranging conversation, some of which is captured within this volume. And of course, none of this would have been possible without the unconditional support and care I received from my family: this book and all my work is dedicated to you.

I will end as I began, with an annotation about Wafaa. Not every artist harbors a hard-won conviction about the role of the artist in society, but Wafaa is not every artist. As he observed early in the process of developing this book, it is imperative that the role of the artist evolves to meet our moment: "A mirror that only reflects things is not enough anymore. What's required is a mirror with a conscience. And that is what the artist is." This is exactly what Wafaa offers us through his work.

Bana Kattan
Pamela Alper Associate Curator
Museum of Contemporary Art Chicago

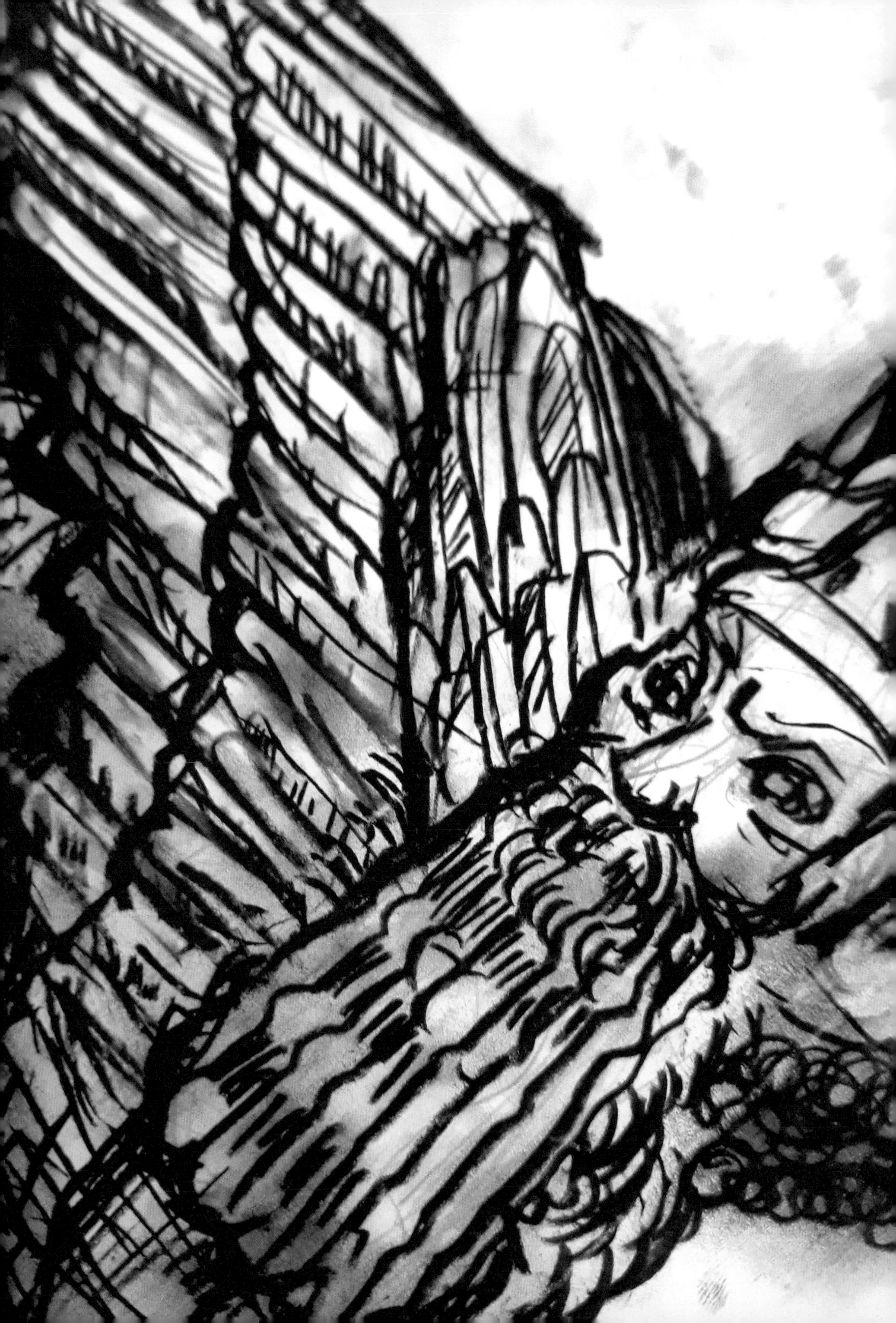

"Cannibalism alone unites us": Wafaa Bilal's Imperatives of Consumption[1]

Bana Kattan

Wafaa Bilal settled in the United States and launched his career as an artist in the late nineties after fleeing Saddam Hussein's Iraq as a political refugee. Not too long after his arrival to the United States, a key narrative about the Muslim world was beginning to form. In 2001, following the attacks on September 11 and the subsequent invasion of Afghanistan, the Middle East was effectively set up as the enemy and the locale for the so-called war on terror. This narrative was fueled by the legality of racial profiling, which gave the US government official permission to treat Arabs as suspects, creating a wave of "cultural racism" based on the logic of "othering."[2] In 2003, Bilal found himself experiencing the side effects of this shift while having to watch the United States invade his country from afar. He was physically distant from the violence unfolding at home, yet he remained emotionally and psychologically bound to its effects. Whether it was racist remarks from people in the United States or the actual pangs of familial and cultural loss resultant from the war abroad, Bilal found himself in a corrosive cultural power dynamic. It is this dynamic, and in particular the imbalance of power between the United States and Iraq, that informs much of his practice.

Caught between an unwelcoming present and a violently destroyed past, Bilal has turned to artistic projects that reflect, or in his words, "turn a mirror to," this condition. From early works that engage bodily performance and technology to more recent ones that embrace science and the poetic gesture, Bilal's innovative and interdisciplinary approaches reveal the tensions at play in existing within a cultural power (e.g., the United States), whose history and contemporary politics are based in colonial and interventionist strategies. In another sense, his work is an interrogation of what it means to be consumed and what it means to live within the world of the consumer. This might also be described as a form of "cultural cannibalism," which for the purposes of this essay is defined as a source of cultural consumption, or appropriation, that seeks to destroy, retain, assimilate, or exploit. When applied to Bilal's practice, it becomes quickly evident that cultural cannibalism, in this sense of the phrase, has been a central (albeit largely unconscious) concern of his, and it shows up repeatedly in his work.

The concept of cultural cannibalism isn't new. For one, it has long been embedded in decolonization and assimilation metaphors in the work of Native American artists. On this topic, artist Andrea Carlson has authored a particularly

1. The main title of this essay quotes the first line of Oswald de Andrade's "Cannibalist Manifesto," trans. Leslie Bary, *Latin American Literary Review* 19, no. 38 (July/December 1991): 38–47.
2. Nadine Naber, "'Look, Mohammed the Terrorist is Coming!': Cultural Racism, Nation-Based Racism, and the Intersectionality of Oppressions after 9/11," in *Race and Arab Americans before and after September 11th: From Invisible Citizens to Visible Subjects*, eds. Amaney Jamal and Nadine Naber (Syracuse, NY: Syracuse University Press, 2007), 279.

constructive text. Writing about her work *Sunshine on a Cannibal* (2015), she notes: "Cannibalism as a colonial-created subject, is the ultimate *other*, the non-colonized or the un-civilizable. . . . The cannibal of this work is those forces who assimilate, conquer, and proselytize, but also supplant other narratives with all-consuming frameworks."[3] Through her work, Carlson highlights this hypocrisy—that just as Western oppressors were pointing at Indigenous peoples and labeling them as cannibals, they were authorizing the consumption of Native America and its lands.

The language of cannibalism was similarly embraced by proponents of Brazilian modernism starting in the 1920s and again in the 1960s, when the art movement Tropicália revitalized the "cannibalist" narrative laid out by their modernist predecessors. This narrative, popularized by the poet Oswald de Andrade in his 1928 *Manifesto Antropófago*, centered on the concept of *antropofagia* (or anthropophagy), which challenged Western power structures by transforming the act of cannibalism into "a willful aggressive form of creativity, nourishment, and strength."[4] By selectively appropriating and subsuming aspects of European culture into their own work, artists involved in the Tropicália movement, including Hélio Oiticica, Lygia Clark, and Rogério Duarte, were asserting independence over European colonial culture.

Interestingly, Andrea Carlson herself has noted the potential applications of the Brazilian modernist writing on cannibalism—"as a political vehicle, as a disruptor, and how they're using it to be transgressive"—and has even adopted this approach in her own work.[5] In her *VORE* series of paintings, for instance, Carlson populates her imagined landscapes with objects from encyclopedic collections (the Minneapolis Institute of Art and the British Museum specifically), and text references from exploitation films, many of which include the word "cannibal" in their titles and tag lines. Revealing and building off this pretense, I would argue that Bilal, like Carlson and the group of Brazilian artists and thinkers before them, mobilizes and inverts the cannibalistic narrative previously dominated by the West to both challenge and embrace it. He is, in this sense, operating within a particular art historical lineage whose concern seems to be whether cannibalism, as an artistic device, can be deployed to interrogate Western cultural practices and patterns. For Bilal, this concern finds expression in both the form and content of his work.

3. Andrea Carlson, "A Note on 'Sunshine on a Cannibal,'" *Andrea Carlson* (blog), March 26, 2017, https://www.mikinaak.com/blog/a-note-on-sunshine-on-a-cannibal-and-indigenious.
4. Santiago Colás, "From Caliban to Cronus: A Critique of Cannibalism as Metaphor for Cuban Revolutionary Culture," in *Eating Their Words: Cannibalism and the Boundaries of Cultural Identity*, ed. Kristen Guest (Albany: State University of New York Press, 2001), 130.
5. Andrea Carlson, interviewed by Olivia von Gries, and quoted in Olivia von Gries, "The Consumed Bite Back: Issues of Cultural Cannibalism and Appropriation in Andrea Carlson's *Windigo* and *VORE* Series" (master's thesis, University of Oklahoma, 2021), 30, https://shareok.org/handle/11244/329605.

Arguably, the most direct way Bilal engages with this notion of cultural cannibalism is through the use of his body in performance. By centering his body and making it available for public display and, in some cases, audience interaction, he is placing the viewer in a direct relationship with himself and the work, thus making them complicit in the actions or outcomes of the performance. He uses this dynamic with his audience "to reverse [the] process of disengagement," which is a tendency he sees people fall into when political conflicts feel far away.[6] For this reason, he chooses to rely on interactive models that require spectator participation to generate or complete the work. He explains this impetus, saying: "I'm very interested in communication that allows audience participation to become a component of the projects I initiate, which means the narrative is open and participants can assign any meaning to it, and, at the end, [they] become part of it."[7] One of the earliest examples of this participatory activation is his 2007 durational performance work *Domestic Tension* (pp. 50–57). Repurposing Chicago's FlatFile Gallery into a living space outfitted with a robotic paintball gun, Bilal confined himself there for thirty-one days and invited audiences to shoot at him over the internet. Viewers were granted twenty-four-hour access to a live feed, which allowed them to track his movements and fire the paintball gun at will. Over the course of the thirty-one days, about 65,000 shots were fired by shooters from 136 different countries.

Bilal was inspired to make *Domestic Tension* after he learned the devastating news that his brother, Haaji, was killed in Iraq in 2004 by a drone strike facilitated remotely from a US military base. Bilal's *Domestic Tension* performance not only challenged the existence of the Iraq War and the use of drone artillery, but it also included an online chat room that exposed the darkness of many internet users and their online spaces (which are often places of presumed anonymity).[8] As part of the project, Bilal also uploaded daily video logs narrating the difficulties of his day-to-day experience, which, combined with his multipronged approach to online viewer interaction via live stream and chat, created a participatory environment more complex than the relatively basic invitation of shoot or don't shoot. Indeed, the project compelled audiences to consider the ways they themselves were implicated in state-sanctioned violence through the same technology

6. Anjali Kamat, "Interview with Iraqi Artist Wafaa Bilal," *Arab Studies Journal* 18, no. 1 (2010): 324. http://www.jstor.org/stable/27934088.
7. Kamat, "Interview with Iraqi Artist Wafaa Bilal," 320.
8. See the opening and closing pages of this volume for examples from the *Domestic Tension* chat log.

that typically delivers said violence. It also highlighted how passive spectatorship infers complicity as does the most obvious act of firing the gun.

In *Cannibal Culture: Art, Appropriation, and the Commodification of Difference*, author Deborah Root warns that it is the conceptual art systems that are "abstracted from their social and cultural matrix, imagined as something separate and transcendent that makes all the violence and repressions of history thinkable."[9] What Bilal brings us back to with *Domestic Tension* is an art system that makes those realities of violence and repression not only "thinkable," but tangible. On one level, the performance acts as a reflection of both the contemporary geopolitics of the moment and humanity's base impulses. On another level, it can be seen as part of a political, societal, and historical continuum of consumption of marginalized bodies. Bilal has commented to this effect:

> It reminds me of the days I was [performing] *Domestic Tension*. . . . All that people wanted was to entertain themselves, to indulge themselves. I was invisible to them. I think that's where, to me, the interpretation of cultural cannibalism is. In order for one culture to survive, that culture thinks it has to consume the other culture, which is not true at all. It could coincide with, it could co-live with, but there is a misconception you have to destroy the other in order to live above.[10]

On its surface, the physical and mental risk taken by Bilal in *Domestic Tension* recalls Chris Burden's performance *Shoot* (1971), wherein the artist arranged to have himself shot by a friend in a gallery space in Santa Ana, California. Burden's intentions behind the piece were to reflect how commonplace the idea of being shot had become in the United States during the Vietnam War. An extreme yet essential entry into the canon of protest art, *Shoot* can certainly be read in line with this notion of cannibalization and the body, especially as a function of political protest. However, considering some key differences between the two performances—such as the anonymity and number of Bilal's shooters, the extended nature and multimodal forms of abuse inflicted on Bilal, and, perhaps most notably, the centrality of his identity as an Iraqi, Muslim man—I find it equally if not more productive to relate *Domestic Tension* to Yoko Ono's consequential *Cut Piece* (1964), in which Ono sat silently on stage and invited visitors to cut away pieces of her clothing using a pair of scissors.

9. Deborah Root, *Cannibal Culture: Art, Appropriation, and the Commodification of Difference* (New York: Routledge, 2018), 18.
10. Wafaa Bilal, "Interview with the Artist," exhibition video, *Wafaa Bilal: Indulge Me*, Museum of Contemporary Art Chicago, January 10, 2024.

Ono first preformed *Cut Piece* in Japan before staging it in New York, London, and Paris. While all the performances are difficult to watch, the ones presented to Western audiences were particularly unnerving and grossly accentuated the aspects of her work that addressed gender-based violence, objectification, and the exotification of her identity as a Japanese American woman. In New York in particular, there was little hesitation on the part of the audience to participate, and the silent stoicism of Ono was often disrupted by laughter from the crowd (not to mention the notably crude cutting choices from many of the male participants). By the end of the New York performance, the physical and emotional strain on the artist is clearly evident as a tear rolls down her cheek. Despite the differing historical and gender contexts of the two performances, similar physical and emotional pressures can be seen in Bilal's daily video documentation during the run of *Domestic Tension*. And like Ono, the damage inflicted on Bilal isn't necessarily limited to the physical discomfort or fear resultant from the performance. Rather, it extends to the dissolution of his identity as an objectified, so-called foreign body onto which viewers *act*.

A few years after *Domestic Tension*, Bilal engaged in yet another durational and painful performance, this time one that would last more than an entire calendar year. Like *Domestic Tension*, Bilal's *3rdi* (2010–11; pp. 64–75) sees the artist engage in self-cannibalization by offering his body for public consumption. For the work, Bilal surgically implanted a camera into the back of his skull and programmed it to take minute-by-minute photographs of whatever was behind him. Over the course of a year, internet users could track his life (or rather, the life of the world around him) through the project website, where the images were directly uploaded. Here, internet users were able to both consume the images produced from the back of the artist's head and use the artist's body as an apparatus of surveillance technology—reflecting and in many ways enacting the hypersurveilled world brought forth in the aftermath of 9/11, particularly for Arab and Muslim populations. In the spirit of the Brazilian modernists' take on cannibalism as an appropriation or reversal of Western power, one can interpret Bilal's camera implant as a way of turning his experience as the surveilled into that of the surveillant, upending the usual gaze of US cultural racism.

On a more personal note, *3rdi* reflects, like so many of his works, the artist's longing for an archive of time and place.

Being a refugee has meant that Bilal has almost no photos or records from his youth, a fact that stands in painful contrast to the image-rich and heavily documented world of today. For him, *3rdi* highlights "the places I left behind, none of which I have any record. At the same time I am very interested now in these corners of our lives that we don't pay attention to, how our lives have become so public, and every one of our moves becomes monitored by others."[11] In this way, *3rdi* effectively presses questions of digital surveillance (especially relevant at the time) while responding to the impetus to collect and preserve memories, in particular those memories imperiled by colonial erasure.

SADDAM HUSSEIN AND THE CONSUMPTION OF IRAQ

Another cannibalistic theme taken up by Bilal is that of dictatorship and its relationship to power and egotism. More specifically, Bilal's focus has centered on the dictatorial rule of former Iraqi president Saddam Hussein, whose regime lasted from 1979–2003. Bilal has described life under Saddam Hussein's rule as "living under a regime built on spin and attempted mind control."[12] The spin Bilal is referring to are the various forms of propaganda that were proliferated during his presidency. Hussein had a long history of commissioning public artworks in the form of monuments, billboards, and paintings that connected his persona with ideas and images from the civilizations of ancient Mesopotamia and Babylonia (figs. 1 and 2). Through these works, he presented himself as the embodiment of Iraq, so much so that it can be argued that Hussein used a cannibalistic-style exploitation of Iraqi history, nationalism, and antiquity for his own sociopolitical gain. Eventually, his propaganda provided a visual pretext for the United States' invasion of Iraq and further justification for it after the fact. Author David Simonowitz writes: "In the United States, Iraqi material culture has served as the sign of an evil defeated. The invasion of Iraq was facilitated and subsequently 're-presented' by using Saddam as a screen on which to project an image of a visible, attack-able enemy that stood-in for the invisible, transnational specter of terrorism."[13] In other words, because Hussein saw himself as Iraq, so too did the United States, which meant that destroying Iraq was equivalent to destroying Hussein, and vice versa. Iraqi civilians and their country were a means to an end.

Significant projects in Bilal's oeuvre address and interrogate the production of Hussein's public image. Some, like

11. Kamat, "Interview with Iraqi Artist Wafaa Bilal," 328.
12. Wafaa Bilal, "Invisible Mirror: Aggression and the Thumb-Generation Response," in *We Are Iraqis: Aesthetics and Politics in a Time of War*, eds. Nadje Al-Ali and Deborah Al-Najjar (Syracuse, NY: Syracuse University Press, 2013), 93.
13. David Simonowitz, "Head Trips: An Intertextual Analysis of Later Architecture and Sculpture under Saddam Hussein," *International Journal of Islamic Architecture* 1, no. 1 (2012): 61–81, https://dx.doi.org/10.1386/ijia.1.1.61_1.

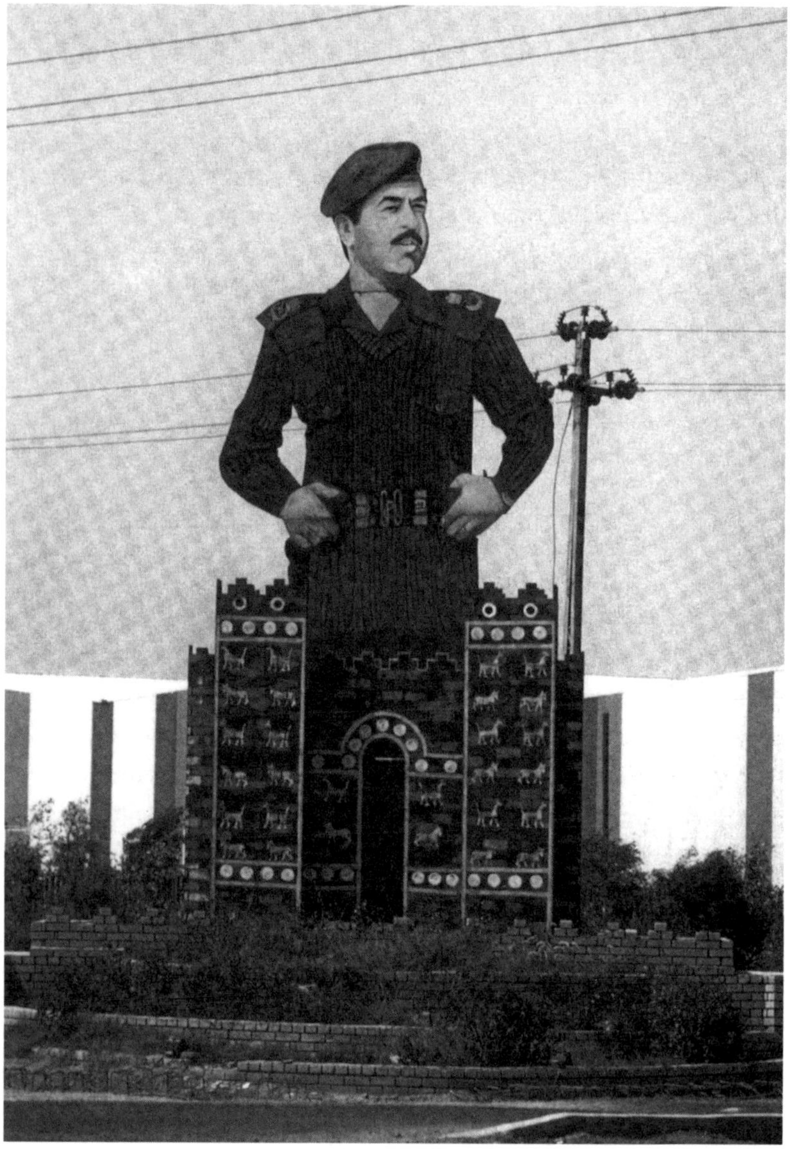

FIGURE 1
Billboard of Saddam Hussein astride the Ishtar Gate, reproduced in Kanan Makiya (a.k.a. Samir al-Khalil), *The Monument: Art, Vulgarity and Responsibility in Iraq* (Berkeley: University of California Press, 1991), page 53, figure 29.

Virtual Jihadi (2008; pp. 58–63), take up the damaging effects of propaganda (particularly on the average Iraqi) as intermediating devices that reinforce stereotypes and provide the aforementioned visual pretext for conflict. Others, such as *Canto III* (2015; p. 77), deal specifically with Hussein's cult of personality, undermining his forceful position as surrogate of Iraqi cultural history and harbinger of national supremacy. The first of these two works, *Virtual Jihadi*, originated from a widely distributed Islamophobic computer game called *The Quest for Saddam* (originally released in 2003 by a US-based amateur game developer), in which players fought stereotypical foes in an attempt to murder Saddam Hussein. Notably, in this original version of the game, every Iraqi has only one face—Hussein's. Three years later, the al-Qaida organization released their own version of the game, titled *The Night of Bush Capturing*,

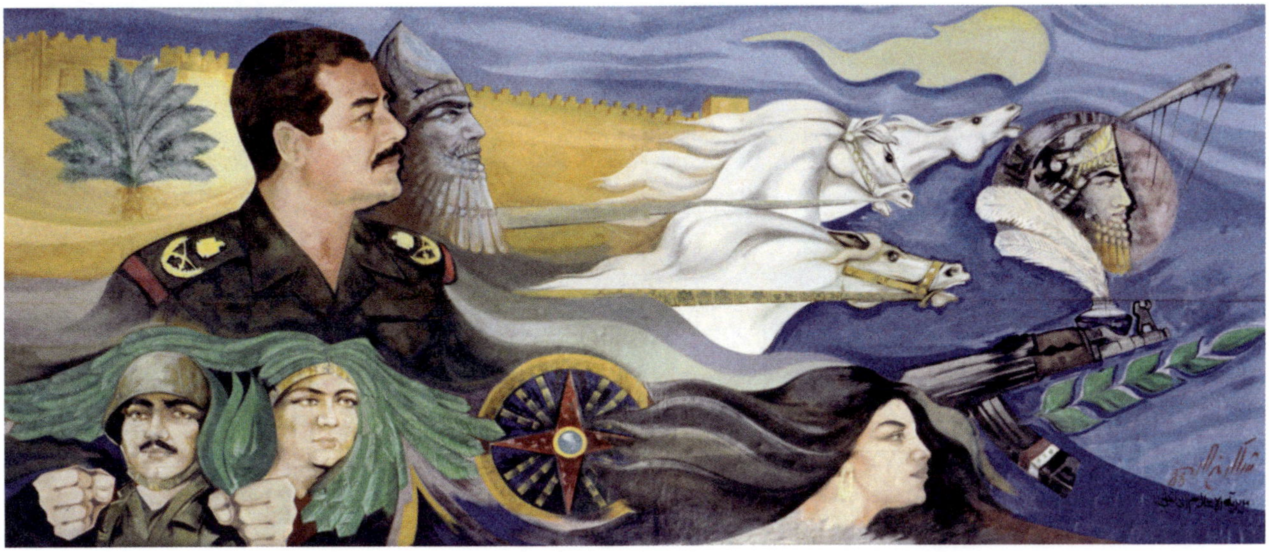

FIGURE 2
Mural on a wall in Iraq equating Saddam Hussein with Nebuchadnezzar, the Babylonian king.

adding a new character skin that turned the goal of the game into a hunt for George W. Bush, who was president of the United States at the time. For his purposes, Bilal saw an opportunity to hack, or reskin, the game for a second time, though his version would place the conflict between the first two games front and center. Leaving in elements from both variants and adding in a new character altogether, Bilal's *Virtual Jihadi* literally and figuratively subsumes the cannibalistic allegory revealed in the making, reskinning, and stealing of the original game, and in doing so underscores the use of appropriation as a tool for social or political messaging.

The newly added character in Bilal's version is an Iraqi suicide bomber, created in the image of the artist himself—once an average civilian who, having become deeply outraged by the killing of his brother in the war, was recruited into a terrorist cell. With this newly added character, Bilal situates both sides—al-Qaida *and* the US military—as the enemy, bringing attention to the ways his generation in Iraq has largely been defined by war, both as victims of recruitment by violent groups and as casualties of US intervention. In Bilal's game, the average Iraqi is the one who pays the highest price. Of course, the fact of it being a video game should not be overlooked. Like many of Bilal's projects, what at first reads like a playful invitation is actually a vehicle for deeper meaning and engagement that considers topics including the use of technology to sanitize war, the popularization of video games as military recruiting tools, and the comfortable distance that modern day weaponry creates from the reality of harm. In this instance, Bilal invites participants to join in a first-person shooter game, but as their play progresses and as they understand the implications of their actions in relation to the images on the screen, they're brought to reckon with the inescapable travesties the war has wrought on the culture and identity of Iraq.

The history of the exhibition and display of *Virtual Jihadi* became yet another way of expanding the ideas already emergent in the work. In March 2008, *Virtual Jihadi* was set to be exhibited at Rensselaer Polytechnic Institute in Troy, New York, but due to complaints from the college's Republican club, the exhibition was hastily closed. When an independent media venue, the Sanctuary, offered a space for the work, it was again shut down, this time by city officials. Bilal perfectly summarizes the experience, saying: "Even though it's a video game and everybody understands it's a video game the Rensselaer Polytechnic Institute decided to cancel the show and the FBI, CIA, and Homeland Security all showed up on the show's opening night. In 2003 there was no public objection to the original [US-made] video game. It became objectionable only when I hacked the game and the hunter became the hunted."[14] This statement by Bilal brings to mind the kind of cultural cannibalism espoused by Tropicália artists who advocated for the appropriation of Western culture for their own purposes, on their own terms. In Bilal's case, he took what was originally a propaganda tool created in the United States to fight the war on terror (represented, of course, by the pervasive visage of Hussein), and later stolen by al-Qaida for their own propagandist aims, and made it into something that reflected his own experience as an Iraqi man, caught in the middle of a simulated war on screen.

Many writers have reflected on Saddam Hussein's megalomania and the use, by both him and his Ba'ath Party, of monumentality to scaffold his power. Yet, none of the examples are more quintessential than the unfulfilled tribute planned by the Ba'ath Party to send a bust of their honored ruler into space. The intent was for the Iraqi Space Program to launch sculptures of Hussein into space, geosynchronized to hover above Iraq, with the hopes that they would become stars in the sky shining down on Iraq for eternity. For Bilal, this was "a reminder of the dictator's eye looking upon you and watching you."[15] Inspired by this outlandish plan, Bilal created a series of works that examine Saddam Hussein's virtuosic performance of power, the first being the antimonument work *Canto III*.[16] For the work, Bilal created a golden bust of Hussein inspired by four identical, nine-meter-high sculptures

14. Kamat, "Interview with Iraqi Artist Wafaa Bilal," 321.
15. Bilal, "Interview with the Artist."
16. The title of Bilal's sculpture, *Canto III*, is named after the third canto of Lord Byron's *Childe Harold's Pilgrimage* (1812–18), in which the protagonist reflects on violence, sorrow, and remembrance. It contains memorable stanzas that assess the value of fame, such as Death ought to "unteach mankind the lust to shine or rule" (stanza 43).

that once embellished the Qasr al-Salam, or Peace Palace, of the former president. The sculptures portray Hussein from the chest up in full military regalia. On his shoulders sit a series of medals and a braided sash. Finally, and most importantly, on his head there rests a helmet-shaped replica of the Dome of the Rock in Jerusalem—the oldest existing example of Islamic architecture and one of the most well-known religious sites in the world, particularly important both historically and spiritually to the Islamic faith. In addition to presenting himself as the embodiment of Iraq, the adornment of the Dome reveals Hussein's aim to associate himself as a Pan-Arab hero.

Canto III has become the basis for various other replica busts, including ones the artist has made into commercial goods such as candlestick holders and bookends. Most recently, however, Bilal has deployed another version of *Canto III* that directly engages with the unrealized dream of a monument to Hussein in space. Made especially for the MCA exhibition, this realization of Hussein's gold bust, titled *Thumbsat Model* (2024; p. 82), takes the form of a tiny, one-inch replica affixed to a model satellite, which will be launched into space on the occasion of this exhibition's opening. Unlike the original plan by the Ba'ath Party, Bilal's bust will be placed in low orbit, making its lifespan circling the Earth temporary. Eventually, the device will fall and be destroyed as it reenters Earth's atmosphere. Bilal explains his desire for the sculpture's journey to end in this way: "Disintegrating into ashes in the atmosphere. I thought that is a beautiful poetic ending to an era that we do not want to see again."[17]

The literal incineration of Hussein's sculpture (itself a consuming action), in addition to Bilal's repeat use of appropriation (this time of Hussein's own iconography), points to ways the artist may be thinking about consumption as a conversion, or rectifying, tactic. In other words, taking the power of a tyrannical ruler, represented here in the form of a golden bust sent into space, and transforming it into its opposite: a humorously diminutive expression of the failure of that power to rule, to endure. In this way, the work, like others in Bilal's oeuvre, can be read as a cannibalizing of totalitarian power to, in turn, generate artistic power.

The timing of the artist's *Thumbsat Model* project invites another layer of meaning. Intended to coincide with his exhibition at the MCA in 2025, the launch of Bilal's satellite is planned to take place amid an ongoing and rapidly

17. Bilal, "Interview with the Artist."

expanding space race happening among billionaire capitalists—namely, Elon Musk, Jeff Bezos, and Richard Branson. The extraplanetary undertakings of these three billionaires are creating a resurgence in space activity second only to that of 1957, when the Soviet Union's successful launch of Sputnik 1 began the world's first space race. Of course, that race was supposedly won when the United States' first crewed spacecraft landed on the moon in 1969. Although there has yet to be a so-called victor in today's corporate space race, the key historic parallel that can be drawn between then and now is the competition itself—public figures aiming for attention by demonstrating supremacy and domination over the opposition: In July 2021, in the midst of a global pandemic, Richard Branson took a ninety-minute trip, fifty miles into Earth's atmosphere. Ten days later, Jeff Bezos flew out on a ten-minute tour surpassing Branson's distance to reach the Kármán line, largely recognized as the edge of space. Then, in September, Elon Musk's SpaceX launched into Earth's orbit for a three-day tour. Each launch outdid the other, whether in time or distance traveled.

In her book *Astrotopia: The Dangerous Religion of the Corporate Space Race*, Professor Mary-Jane Rubenstein draws a link between humans' interactions with space exploration and fifteenth-century European settlers' use of Judeo-Christian concepts to justify their destruction of Indigenous ecosystems: "The escalating effort to colonize the cosmos is a renewal of the religious, political, economic, and scientific maelstrom that globalized Earth beginning in the fifteenth century."[18] Indeed, while it is sometimes subtle, the language and symbolism used by Musk, Bezos, and Branson to describe their ventures indicate the exploitative, colonialist, and capitalist motivations behind this new race. Their web pages, for example, are populated with words and phrases such as "pioneering," "for the good of mankind," or "the new frontier."[19] Just as landing on the moon was a sign of national power and supremacy in 1969, the same is true today for billionaires seeking dominion beyond Earth's surface (fig. 3).

Certainly, this ostentatious pursuit of extraplanetary supremacy is not too dissimilar to how the Ba'ath Party intended for their own leader to occupy space. Where once Saddam Hussein used Iraq and its history for social and political gain on Earth, the unrealized plan to send his bust to space to exist as a star for eternity extended that political

18. Mary-Jane Rubenstein, *Astrotopia: The Dangerous Religion of the Corporate Space Race* (Chicago, IL: University of Chicago Press, 2024), x.
19. Richard Branson's Virgin Galactic uses both colonial and savior language by suggesting their undertaking will "*pioneer* this exciting new space age for *humanity*" and "benefit . . . humankind" (emphasis added). Virgin Galactic, https://www.virgin.com/virgin-companies/virgin-galactic. Similarly, Jeff Bezos's Blue Origin uses the central tag line: "For the benefit of Earth." Bezos has even spoken fondly of space settler colonialism while encouraging the use of space resources, saying: "I would love to see a trillion humans living in the solar system. . . . We can easily support a civilization that large with all of the resources in the solar system. . . . We will take materials from the moon and from near-Earth objects . . . and so on, and we'll build giant O'Neill style colonies and people will live in those." Transcript for Jeff Bezos: Amazon and Blue Origin, *Lex Fridman Podcast* no. 405, https://lexfridman.com/jeff-bezos-transcript/#chapter2_space. Elon Musk, too, has blatantly professed a similar goal for his company: "one day, we will indeed occupy Mars." Elon Musk at Starbase, January 12, 2024, https://www.teslaoracle.com/2024/01/16/elon-musks-spacex-achievements-in-2023-starship/.

FIGURE 3
Elon Musk wearing an "Occupy Mars" shirt at a SpaceX event in Boca Chica Beach, Texas, 2022.

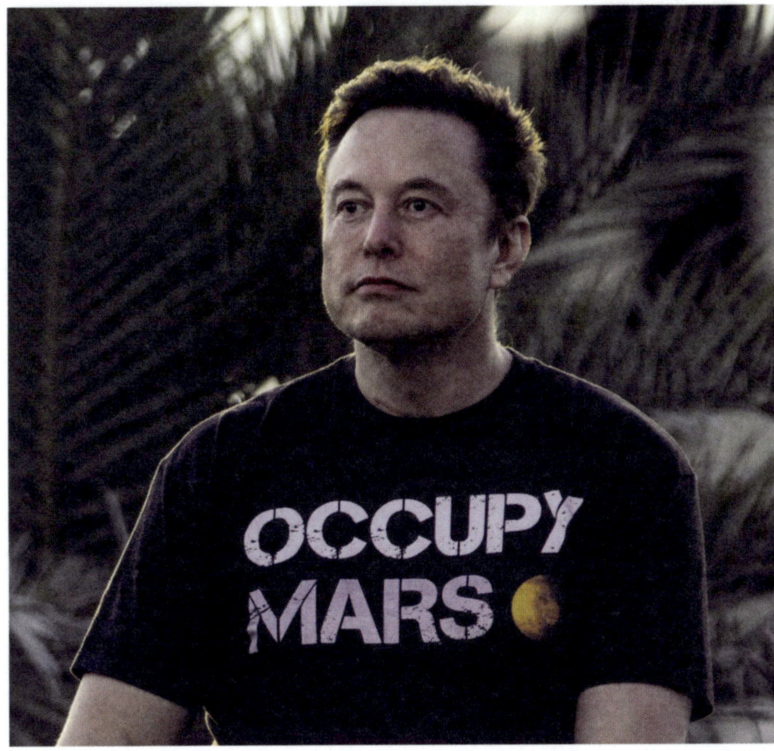

reach ever skyward. Bilal's performative gesture of placing Hussein in space with *Thumbsat Model* poetically pulls it all together. Except this time, it's on the artist's own terms: the ego of Hussein, and whoever else his megalomania represents, is combated by the splendor of a single, miniature bust launched into space only to eventually crash and burn. Bilal consumes, both to upset the power structure and to create a sense of distinction between himself and Western cannibalism.

THE CANNIBALIZATION OF HISTORY

Sadly, Saddam Hussein was not the only cannibalistic culprit in Iraq, nor was he the lone focus of Bilal's interrogation of his country's long history of destruction. Iraq has endured centuries of devastation to its land, people, and material culture, from the Mongols who set fire to the storied House of Wisdom in the thirteenth century, to the terrorist group ISIS who enacted their brutal campaign of cultural erasure in the 2010s, to the US-led invasion of Iraq in the twenty-first century.[20] The country has also endured other, more indirect forms of destruction, in particular those resulting from the appropriation and orientalization of Iraq by Western interlopers. An unexpected example of this form of cultural cannibalization comes from architect Frank Lloyd Wright and his history with the country. In the mid-1950s,

20. Since the 2003 invasion of Iraq, over 600,000 ancient archeological artifacts have been illegally removed from Iraq, its museums, and excavation sites. See Lawrence Rothfield, *The Rape of Mesopotamia: Behind the Looting of the Iraq Museum* (Chicago, IL: University of Chicago Press, 2009). As for destruction, the United States and other coalition military armies chose to build one of their primary bases on the sites of ancient Babylon and Ur, causing serious, irreversible damage. Though the Polish government later apologized for its complicity, the US government, who was leading the faction, has yet to apologize.

Wright and several other famous architects at the time were invited to Baghdad by the Iraqi government to help refashion the metropolis as a modern city. Wright was originally tasked with designing a grand opera and civic auditorium, which was to include a museum and library. During his site visit, however, Wright convinced the Iraq Development Board to expand his purview. In addition to the opera house, Wright proposed his "Plan for Greater Baghdad," which included landscaped parks, museums, commercial bazaars, and a circular campus for the university. The many gardens and ornamental flourishes scattered throughout Wright's master plan—including a proposal for a statue of Aladdin and his lamp to sit atop the opera house—highlighted a decidedly Western fixation with Arab history and symbolism (fig. 4). Even though the project in Iraq was never realized, the vision of decorative camels, Aladdin imagery, and other such features made it, as leading architectural critic Nicolai Ouroussoff has argued, "an embarrassing example of Western chauvinism."[21]

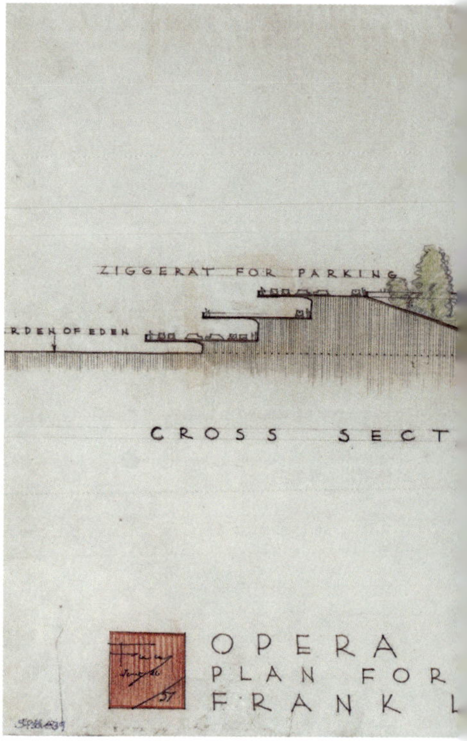

Where this example points to culturally appropriative practices on the part of Western ideology, another culprit of Iraq's physical and cultural erosion comes in the form of internal ideological conflict, which has resulted in the deliberate targeting of cultural artifacts. In 2014 and 2015, for example, ISIS intentionally destroyed neo-Assyrian relics to announce their political arrival on the world stage. One of the more notable pieces destroyed by ISIS was the winged bull of Nineveh—a protective deity that is part bull, part eagle, part human—that once flanked the entrance to the ancient city. This particular act of annihilation is the focus of one of Bilal's newest projects, *In a Grain of Wheat* (2023–25; pp. 86, 88–90), which at its core aims to rectify ISIS's act of cultural destruction.

For this elaborate conceptual project, Bilal began working with Assyrian lamassu sculptures housed at the Metropolitan Museum of Art in New York (pp. 84–85). The Met has a pair of lamassus originally from Nimrud, which had been excavated from an archeological site by Europeans in the 1840s, sold, and ultimately gifted to the museum by J. D. Rockefeller in the early 1930s. The first step in Bilal's *In a Grain of Wheat* project required the artist to generate a very detailed 3D scan of one of the sculptures. Working with a small team of collaborators and using cutting-edge biological engineering and imagining techniques, Bilal then compressed the massive file to a small enough size where it could be embedded into the DNA of

21. Nicolai Ouroussoff, "When Iraq Looked West," *Los Angeles Times*, December 14, 2003, https://www.latimes.com/la-ca-ouroussoff14dec14-story.html; and, Neil Levine, *The Architecture of Frank Lloyd Wright* (Princeton, NJ: Princeton University Press, 1996), 383–404.

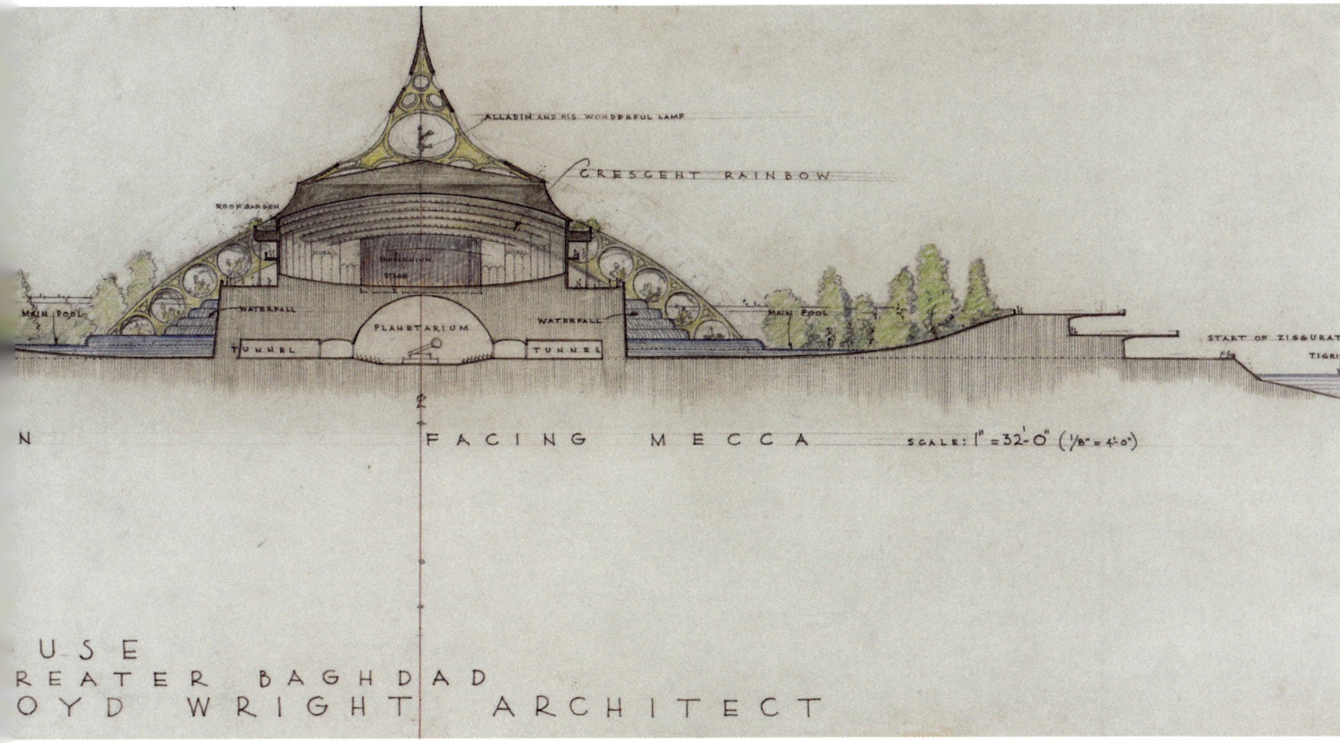

FIGURE 4
Frank Lloyd Wright, *Project 5733: Plan for Greater Baghdad (Baghdad, Iraq). Crescent Opera, Unbuilt Project*, 1957. Architectural drawing: pencil, colored pencil, ink on paper; 16 1/4 × 42 3/4 in. (41.3 × 108.6 cm). The Frank Lloyd Wright Foundation Archives (The Museum of Modern Art | Avery Architectural and Fine Arts Library, Columbia University).

a wheat seed. Bilal selected wheat grains specifically because they were one of the first crops domesticated by humans in the very same region where the winged bull of Nineveh was sculpted.

In *Wafaa Bilal: Indulge Me*, these modified seeds will be installed spilling out of the hoof of a seven-foot-tall, 3D-printed replica of the lamassu commissioned by the MCA, titled *Lamassu (In a Grain of Wheat)* (2025; pp. 87 and 90). Visitors will be encouraged to bow down in front of the sculpture and take a grain of wheat—a reverential act that functions both as a simulated ritual mourning the loss of the original lamassu and as a symbolic offering to its afterlife as a reproducible and indestructible bio-digital surrogate (pp. 92–93). Each grain holds a record of an invaluable piece of Iraqi culture able to be propagated, cultivated, and ultimately consumed. As the artist has offered: "How do we save our antiquities, make them invisible to the enemy yet accessible to us and the generation that follows?"[22] In the midst of ongoing threats to Iraq's material heritage, this artwork provides an answer in the form of in vitro DNA data storage technology, bolstering efforts in cultural preservation by using nature's first archive to transform terrorist violence into restorative agency.

As bio-archiving—or the archival storage of biological data—makes new practices of cultural documentation

22. Bilal, "Interview with the Artist."

and communication possible, and as those technologies become increasingly accessible, could the writing of data onto DNA become a new form of creative expression? Bilal's work seems to suggest so. Whether we write it onto DNA or inscribe it into clay or onto a scroll, encoded cultural memory is the algorithm that moves humanity forward. Bilal suggests that like Gilgamesh five thousand years on, the concept of everlasting life is still at play—even if the double helix is now part digital.

—

Much of Bilal's work comes as a cautionary tale, often drawing on lessons from the past as a forewarning for the future. Whether it is the death of his brother or the demolition of Iraqi heritage, Bilal bears witness to the personal and collective suffering brought on by generations of conflict. Through his work, he reveals the physical, psychological, and cultural damage such suffering has wrought, and in turn shows us that it will continue if these past and present tragedies are left unacknowledged and unheeded. His engagement with these difficult narratives has usually come at the expense of his own health and well-being. He has been shot at repeatedly, undergone elective cranial surgery, endured a seemingly endless stream of racism, and navigated many politically dangerous situations. In some sense, he has made himself and his art a vehicle for collective pain, providing a way for an increasingly distracted or inattentive public to emotionally or physically confront subjects they might otherwise look away from. In doing so, he asks people to reckon with their relationship both to him and the subjects his work represents. This bringing to account, while often predicated on the artist's own hardship and harm, has been a way for Bilal to take back power.

As he has asked people to consume his work, he has in turn revealed to them the fact of their consumption. In this way, he is enacting, or at the very least representing, a kind of cultural cannibalism that, like the Tropicália artists before him, is as generative as it is informative. To be sure, he is showing us the way the world is—through uncomfortable confrontations with pain, loss, and seemingly unresolvable conflicts—but he is also endeavoring to realize a more promising future. He aims for a postconflict ideal, one informed by an aesthetics of conscience and empathy.

Over the first half of Bilal's *Domestic Tension* performance, it was difficult to identify much empathy or reflection among its online participants. It was, after all, a game in which they were asked to shoot, and so they did. But as the performance progressed, there was one empathetic online stranger who discovered that by continuously clicking down and to the left, so long as the clicks outnumbered the shooters, you could direct the gun away from Bilal. Working with other strangers from around the world, this user formed what they called a "virtual human shield."[23] By the end of his performance, Bilal addressed his audience, saying the experience "reinforced [his] belief in humanity and human kindness. Thank you so much from keeping the hope alive."[24]

In every one of Bilal's projects, from his earliest artwork critiquing Saddam Hussein that led to his being forced out of Iraq to more recent works challenging viewers to recognize their own apathy and silence, there is defiance. There is also, I would argue, the possibility, if not the outright realization, of hope. It is a kind of hope that is defiant in its expression—daring to persist despite the line of people waiting to shoot.

23. Wafaa Bilal and Kari Lydersen, *Shoot an Iraqi: Art, Life and Resistance Under the Gun* (San Francisco, CA: City Lights, 2008), 142.
24. Wafaa Bilal, "Final Day.. and the gun is silent," posted June 5, 2007, by Wafaa Bilal, YouTube, https://youtu.be/lDZM4Aoo-Ev0?si=BIWWkefrYugimYTP.

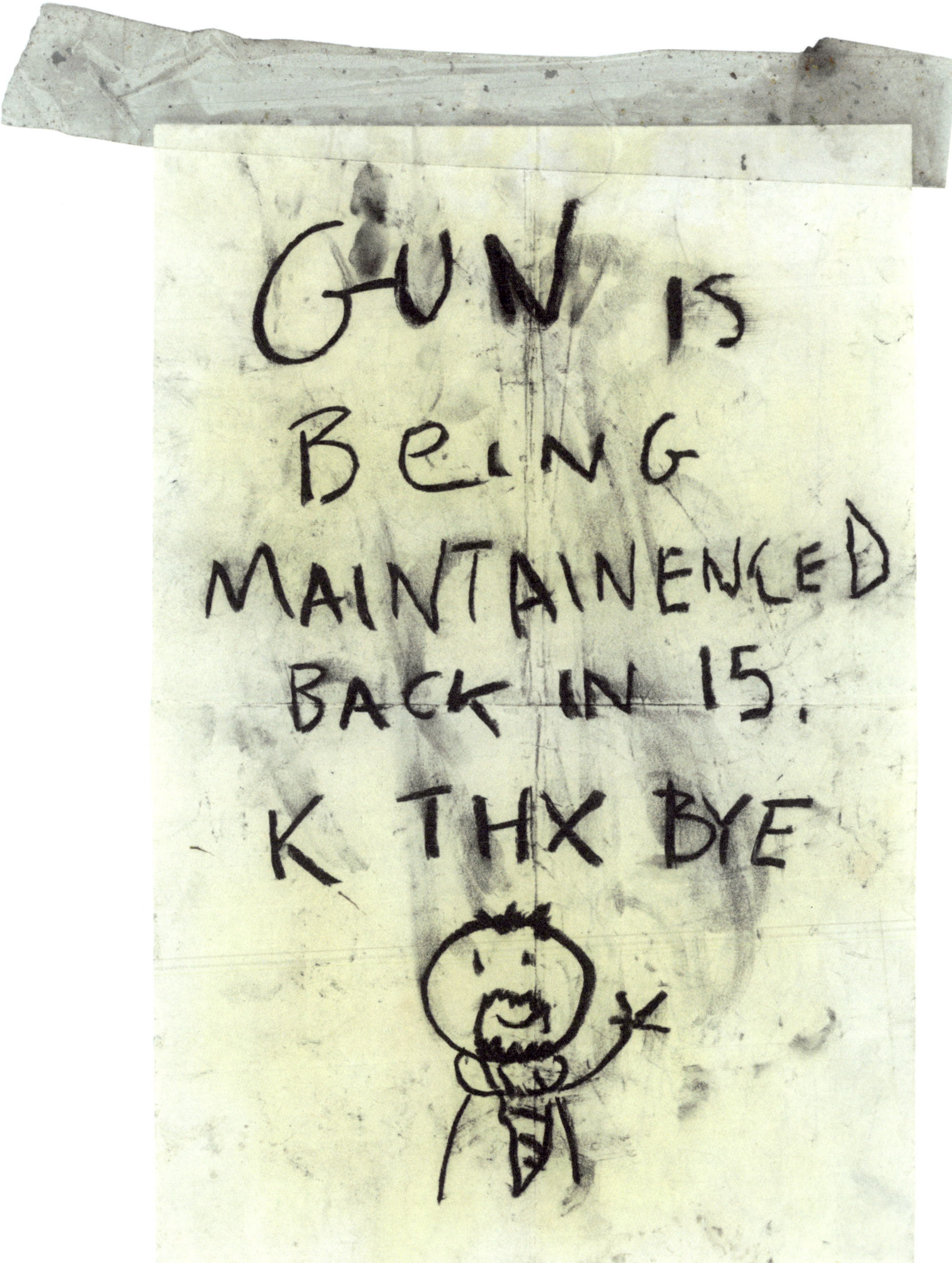
GUN IS
BEING
MAINTAINENCED
BACK IN 15.
K THX BYE

Identifying the Edge of Reality: Wafaa Bilal and Lynn Hershman Leeson in Conversation

Moderated by
Bana Kattan

BANA KATTAN

Wafaa, I'd like to start by discussing your new commissioned piece, *Lamassu (In a Grain of Wheat)* (2025; pp. 87 and 90). It is the work that I would say best connects you to Lynn's practice. The sculptural commission is connected to your earlier project, *In a Grain of Wheat* (2023–25; pp. 86, 88, and 89), which involves embedding a 3D rendering of the recently destroyed, 3,000-year-old winged bull of Nineveh statue into the DNA of a wheat seed. That kind of interdisciplinary engagement between art, science, and technology shares a lot of crossover with the ambitious work Lynn is known for.

WAFAA BILAL

In a Grain of Wheat, as with much of my practice, focuses on reconciling my distance from Iraq. I've thought of myself as the bridge between two places—Iraq, where I existed mentally, emotionally, psychologically, and then the United States, where I existed physically. I was living in the US when the lamassu of Nineveh was destroyed by ISIS in 2015, and it came as such a shock to me and to so many people around the world because it, like so many other cultural artifacts, wasn't just something carved in stone. Cultural products like the lamassu are what hold the stories of our ancestors, and so by destroying it, we are destroying the culture embedded within it, which in turn makes it easier to replace that culture with something else. So, heartbroken by the loss of such a significant piece of cultural production, the first question that came to my mind was whether I could find some way to save it and make it accessible once more and safe from further destruction. The more I pondered that question, the more I came to realize that nature, specifically the structure of DNA, is the first and best storage site we know of. It's a kind of indestructible archive where the essence of everything is written and recorded, and I wanted this poetic element to reinforce the importance of these cultural artifacts.

Once I had that idea, I started looking for a twin replica of the lamassu and was lucky enough to find one at the Met. I contacted them to see if they would collaborate with me, and remarkably they allowed me to generate a full scan of the sculpture, which was great, but at the same time, it was a massive scan. I then began working with scientists to reduce its size so that it could be inserted into the DNA of a wheat plant, which added another layer of poetic meaning to the work, since wheat was one of the first plants people in Mesopotamia domesticated for consumption. The beauty of *In a Grain of Wheat* is you could plant this seed and in a way reverse the process of destruction that befell the lamassu. Now, when you look out at the field, you don't see the lamassu in a literal sense, and yet you know it exists there. It's omnipresent and a part of the nature of things.

BK Lynn, you have similarly described DNA as the perfect archive, especially in the context of your work with antibodies.

LYNN HERSHMAN LEESON Well, all of our history is stored in it. When an infant is born, their DNA holds all the memories of how we became human, going all the way back. DNA also has the potential for adding memory specific to that particular baby, but really it has already recorded all the shifts in DNA that existed up until the child's birth. That's why I always thought of it as an archive, because it's a storage for everything that came before. I once exhibited a piece called *Room #8* (2006–18; fig. 1), the result of a collaboration with scientists at the Swiss pharmaceutical firm Novartis. The piece consists of two vials stored in a mirrored box: One contains a synthetic antibody, the molecular structure of which is encoded with my name, the other contains synthetic DNA encoded with data drawn from my research and from the exhibition. The problem is retrieving all these elements because they're not easy to extract. It takes special equipment to do that.

BK When this work was first exhibited in 2006, do you feel like audiences were able to grasp it? After all, you were showing work that was ahead of its time, and with the way you're describing all of our histories as being embedded into this infinitesimally small thing . . . I'm curious about the audience's reaction.

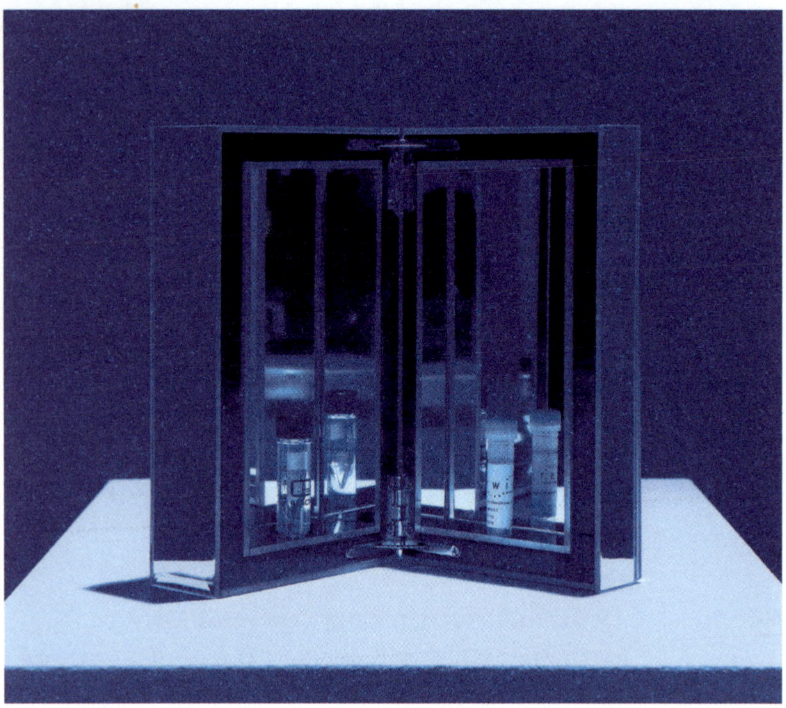

FIGURE 1
Lynn Hershman Leeson, *Room #8*, 2006–18. Lab door, mirror infinity box in blue light, vial of synthetic DNA, vial of LYNNHERSHMAN ANTIBODY, and four digital prints; 85 1/4 × 39 1/4 × 1 5/8 in. (216.5 × 99.7 × 4.1 cm). Collection SFMOMA, Accessions Committee Fund with additional support from Pamela and Richard Kramlich, Kim Anstatt Morton, the Ruth Nash Fund, and purchase, by exchange, through a gift of Peggy Guggenheim.

LHL I'm used to the fact that my artwork is rarely understood in the particular time in which it was created. Generally, it is treated as if nobody understands what I do. Someone may look back twenty years and say, "Oh, that's what she meant," but I don't think there's ever been a time I've shown a work that I considered important and anybody understood it. So, I don't look for an audience to really understand it . . . I wish they would, but at the same time I worry that if they do, they might think that it's not current enough. Ultimately, though, there's never been an appreciation for the ideas I was working with at the time I was working with them. That's true even when I worked with sound.

I don't know if you know this story, but in 1972 I installed a series of my *Breathing Machines* in an exhibition at UC Berkeley's Art Museum. The pieces featured sensors and emitted sound—components that were rarely used in art at the time. Within twenty-four hours, the curator Brenda Richardson closed the exhibition, saying that the work uses sound and sound isn't art. So, the idea that what I do isn't art has been something that's trailed me since for forty-five years. I consider this a good thing, though, because that rejection made me go outside of the museum system, the organized system. Shortly after that exhibition experience in Berkeley, I created site-specific works using hotel rooms and windows to exhibit my work as museums and galleries would not show it. So, I'm really grateful now that that rejection happened. It opened what was possible in terms of art making and display.

WB When I got to the States, I was similarly confronted with the limitations of both plastic art and the ability of galleries and museums to display it. For one thing, I found that those were spaces of privilege, which meant that they privileged access as well. For another, I wanted to build encounters with audiences where there was no set standard for how art should be perceived. For the purposes of my practice, I wasn't necessarily interested in the sort of statement-as-understanding that typically accompanies plastic art, rather I was invested in performance and encounter. I wanted my work to feel like a platform for engagement. That's why when the internet became widely available in the 2000s, I felt it was the perfect time to merge both the physical platform of the gallery with the virtual platform being created online, where you could enter people's homes, offices, and later the palms of their hands. Through that merging, my work became more and more interactive, which also became a way of escaping censorship and gatekeeping.

BK Perhaps we could talk a little bit more about that, considering censorship has had a somewhat significant impact on both of your practices.

WB I think I discovered the power of censorship when I was a student at the University of Baghdad, and I had had a few of my shows closed and confiscated by Saddam's regime. I wasn't really doing much other than mirroring what was happening in Iraq, and I think that's when it dawned on me. Sometimes what we do as artists is mirror a social or political condition, and that might be what scares people most.

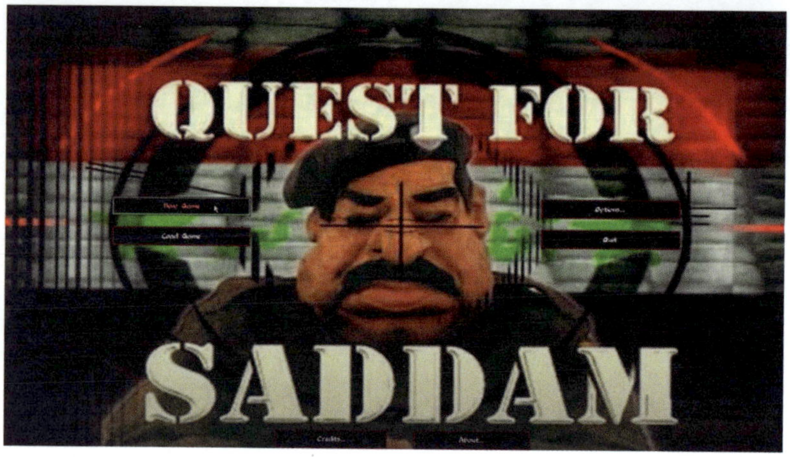

FIGURE 2
Quest for Saddam (still), 2003.

Since my student days, I've been censored multiple times, including in 2008 when Rensselaer Polytechnic Institute in Troy, New York, closed my show, *Virtual Jihadi* (2008; pp. 58–63). Then, once the show was set to open a few days later at a second location, the Sanctuary for Independent Media [also in Troy], the local government closed it down as well, citing building code violations. But, that experience, as much as it was frustrating, highlighted both the power and frustrations of censorship, in that it could help artists as much as it could hurt them. For example, the work at the center of that exhibition, *Virtual Jihadi*, was a video game that was based on another game al-Qaida produced called *The Night of Bush Capturing*, which was a spin-off of a similar game created by an American, Jesse Petrilla, called the *Quest for Saddam* (fig. 2). When the State Department found out about al-Qaida's game, they were outraged about it, saying, "This is propaganda . . . this is a terrorist recruitment tool," but when you downloaded it, it was easy to see how the same criticisms could be levied against Petrilla's original, Islamophobic version. It's just a matter of replacing Saddam with Bush and American soldiers with Iraqi soldiers. Nobody had protested his game, though.

So, for my project, I put myself as the so-called virtual jihadi, simply by changing the skin of the playable character, and once it was shut down by the university and then by the government,

I realized the game needed some form of additional engagement. I decided to call Jesse Petrilla in disguise and tip him off about my work. I said, "Jesse, can you believe this Iraqi guy is taking your game and making it into a jihadi game?" And Jesse went on every radio and TV show he could get on and decried my work, becoming, in a sense, my de facto press person. In that way, I was able to turn what was initially an act of censorship upside down and continue the objective of the art project, which was to expose hypocrisy and racism on a cultural level.

BK — Lynn, you already told us how the Berkley Art Museum took down your work. When else have you dealt with censorship?

LHL — Pretty much everything I have done that is interactive; where viewers interacted directly with the work. Institutions wouldn't show those works because they wouldn't allow things in the museum to be touched. Besides *Lorna* (1979–84), which people really hated, there's not one work that stands out in that way more than the other. Art venues have also refused to show elements of my work. They wouldn't show the DNA. There are so many instances where I've had to revise the idea that I had so that it could be shown in an institution. For a long time I only showed outside of museums or art structures and that was fine. For example, *The Dante Hotel* (1973), which I staged inside of a hotel in North Beach, in San Francisco. Anyone could visit, at any hour of the day, and explore the fictional identity and life of Roberta Breitmore, a character I developed through this and later works. Ultimately it ran for nine months—until it was closed after a visitor called the police, thinking that the body parts of the wax figures I arranged on the hotel bed were real. It was only recently that I started to show within art organizations again.

My very first show in a New York gallery was closed down as the gallery went bankrupt, and I lost everything. Everything was gone. They didn't have insurance at the gallery, and that was the end of it. Another time was in 1998.

I had developed an artificial intelligence chatbot and tried to show it in New York. The work is called *Agent Ruby* (1998–ongoing), and nobody seemed to know what it was at the time. They couldn't understand that you could talk to this thing and it would talk back to you. It is still one of the more advanced chatbots ever made. It's smart and funny, but nobody would write about it. It was rarely even shown at the time, even though it was one of the very first chatbots. But it's now several decades old, and I was making it simultaneous to when AIML, or Artificial Intelligence Markup Language, which is now used to create chatbots, was being written.

BK I wanted to ask you both about the idea of hacking technologies. Wafaa, you touched on this with *Virtual Jihadi* and the changing of the skins within the video game, so perhaps you could talk about the different ways you hack, or incorporate, technology, whether it's a video game or a paintball gun.

WB It goes back to this idea of mirroring. Take *Domestic Tension* (2007; pp. 50–57), for example. In 2004, when I received the terrible news that my brother Haaji was killed by a drone attack in our hometown of Kufa, it took me three years of contemplation to figure out how to communicate that loss with my fellow citizens in the United States. Ultimately, I found inspiration for the piece from a very unlikely source. I was watching ABC News and came across an interview with a drone pilot in Colorado who expressed very little emotional or psychological connection to the people in Iraq, who she was targeting with her drone. I think that was the trigger for me (no pun intended).

I realized I wanted to hold a mirror up to this condition, which in this case meant taking the relevant or related cultural technologies that people in the US would be familiar with, such as paintball, the internet, and the drone, and then reflecting those technologies back onto the culture using a video game–like interface. So, with a couple of faculty and students in the

Art Institute of Chicago basement, we hacked into a paintball gun, then we wrote a bit of software resembling drone software, and then we connected those pieces to the internet. With a camera mounted to the top of the gun, which was in turn pointed at me, we enabled users around the world to experience what it felt like to shoot an Iraqi. Across thirty-one days of twenty-four-hour access, I was shot at over 65,000 times from people all over the world.

I think that's the importance of hacking into an existing system or technology and mirroring it, because the system is already established. You're not asking people to learn anything new. Rather, you are asking them to interact with a thing they already know. So, it was easy for people to interact with the project initially, but later on, as they get into the heart of the piece, they begin to understand the deeper ideas at play. First, you encounter it. It's all fun and games, but then the content seeps in and you begin to ask yourself why is this subject, this person, standing there, receiving hit after hit.

BK For you, Lynn, *America's Finest* (1990–94; fig. 3) comes to mind here, where you hacked an M16 to show video footage of war through its viewfinder, then, if the visitor pulled the trigger, their photo was taken and superimposed onto the crosshairs overlaid on the war footage. There is a significant connection which really drives both works where you and Wafaa are each confronting the viewers with their participation in the violence in front of them.

LHL I have three artworks that use real, special guns that I've had a difficult time showing at public institutions in the United States for years. Nobody would show them. Even *America's Finest*, I tried to include it in my show at the New Museum, but they wouldn't show it. The only place I was able to show *America's Finest* was in Germany and I gave the piece to ZKM [the Center for Art and Media Karlsruhe] so that they would loan it out because it was so hard to get the work back across the border, even with a letter from the State Department. When I showed it, once people cut the cords of it, they took the aggression of a gun and manifested that physically by destroying the work. It really causes a lot of alarm, but it's interesting.

I wanted to show *America's Finest* in Venice as well, but they, too, wouldn't let me show it. They said they didn't want to upset anybody, but when you're dealing with the issues of our culture, it's impossible to ignore the issues the work takes up, especially considering how many people are shot daily in random attacks. So when you deal with the absolute issues of your culture, it can be devastating to have to look at yourself in relation to them, but that is what I think our art should be. If you deal with things that are actually going on and you try to make work that addresses them in some profound way, you're working toward something important. But then that, too, can be silenced. Maybe I'll have to rent a space somewhere and show these works in a way that nobody else will.

BK Basically, we've come full circle. You talked about having to find new locations to show your work early in your career and you're still having to figure that out.

LHL Yeah, and it almost surprises me. I don't understand why. People are so frightened by a project that addresses the lack of humanity of a civilization and the dangers of living there when all they have to do is turn on the news and see it.

WB Culture seems like it's trying to protect itself from itself.

BK I'm wondering if you would both be open to shifting toward science, namely your interests in it and your collaborations with scientists.

LHL Over the past decade alone, I've done several projects with scientists. In 2017 in Switzerland, around the time I was set to have a show at the House of Electronic Arts in Basel [*Lynn Hershman Leeson: Anti-Bodies*, 2018], I wanted to do something with antibodies because Basel was the capital of antibody production. So, I was put in touch with Thomas Huber from Novartis, and we created two antibodies, one called LynnHershman, which became part of *Room #8* and which could bind with anything, and another called (Rob)Erta, which was named after my fictional character Roberta Breitmore and wouldn't bind to anything at all. Roberta's antibody actually proved useful to further scientific research, but the art aspect of those creations was significant because I viewed both as kinds of self-portraits.

Since then, I worked with George Church, a genetics professor at Harvard, who helped me translate some of my past work into binary code that was then converted to DNA. I also recently worked on another project with Thomas Huber called *Twisted Gravity* (2021), which focused on the issue of water pollution. Working with a team at the Wyss Institute at Harvard, we were able to create an installation that actually de-polluted water at a very fast rate using only electricity. As the AquaPulse systems purified the water,

FIGURE 3
Lynn Hershman Leeson, *America's Finest*, 1990–94. Interactive multimedia installation: gun, video camera, loudspeaker, electronics; dimensions variable. Edition of 4 plus II AP. © Lynn Hershman Leeson. Installation view: *Lynn Hershman Leeson: Civic Radar*, ZKM, Karlsruhe, Germany, 2014.

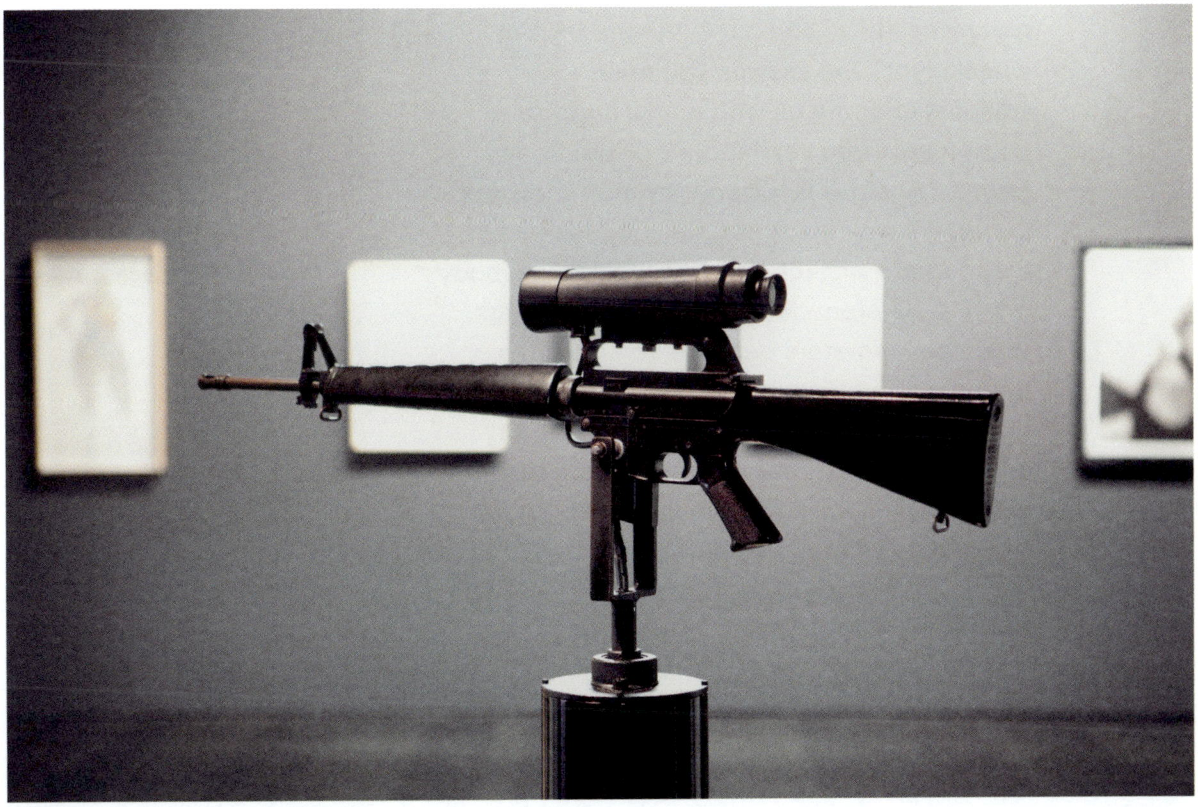

the panels connected to the systems, which featured etched figures of women, would glow in neon.

And, actually, I just finished a new piece with Thomas that's being shown this year. It's an antiaging vaccine, which we had to engineer in China because in the United States and Europe such an experimental vaccine couldn't be made for humans. Back when I made *The Infinity Engine* (2014), which was largely about DNA, I interviewed many of the day's leading scientists, and what's interesting is that so many of them now are interested in death as a disease and antiaging. So, this project for the exhibition *Anti-Aging* (2024), was a way of dealing with that interest in defying death.

WB It sounds like a great project. So, Bana, almost every single project I've made has included a collaborator, because, how I think about it, they're not only bringing the knowledge necessary to make the work possible, they're functioning as a participant, too. Without Ben Chang and Dan Miller, *Domestic Tension* would not be possible. Same thing with *In a Grain of Wheat*. How do you take a scan that is several gigabytes in size and put it into the DNA of a wheat plant? The answer: you need a very good scientist to come up with a new method of compression, so I collaborated with Shawn Lawson. Again, it is not only for their knowledge that I work with these people. It is also for what they add to a project, because I think everybody brings a different dimension to these things. When collaborators become invested in a project and not just outsourced for a job, their ownership leads them to create their own narrative of the work, multiplying the complexities of the story in interesting and unexpected directions.

LHL I agree.

BK Well, Wafaa, wanting to participate in Lynn's vaccine made me realize that I would be remiss to not ask you about using your own body as a subject. Both of your practices include elements of performance, and I'm curious about how you decide what becomes a performance and what doesn't. Relatedly, you've both restaged performances you've done in the past, but in that restaging your body becomes absent, which seems to connect to our ongoing conversation about the archive.

LHL Well, my first thought goes to *Roberta Breitmore* (1973–ongoing; fig. 4), a nine-year performance I did where I assumed the character of Roberta and expanded her personality by way of actual life experiences, allowing her to become more and more real. I kept everything, all the documentation, from those years. I have close to 300 objects in the archive at Stanford where people can go to reperform her life, people who are trying to understand who she is because she doesn't exist in the same way that she did then. That project was really about identifying

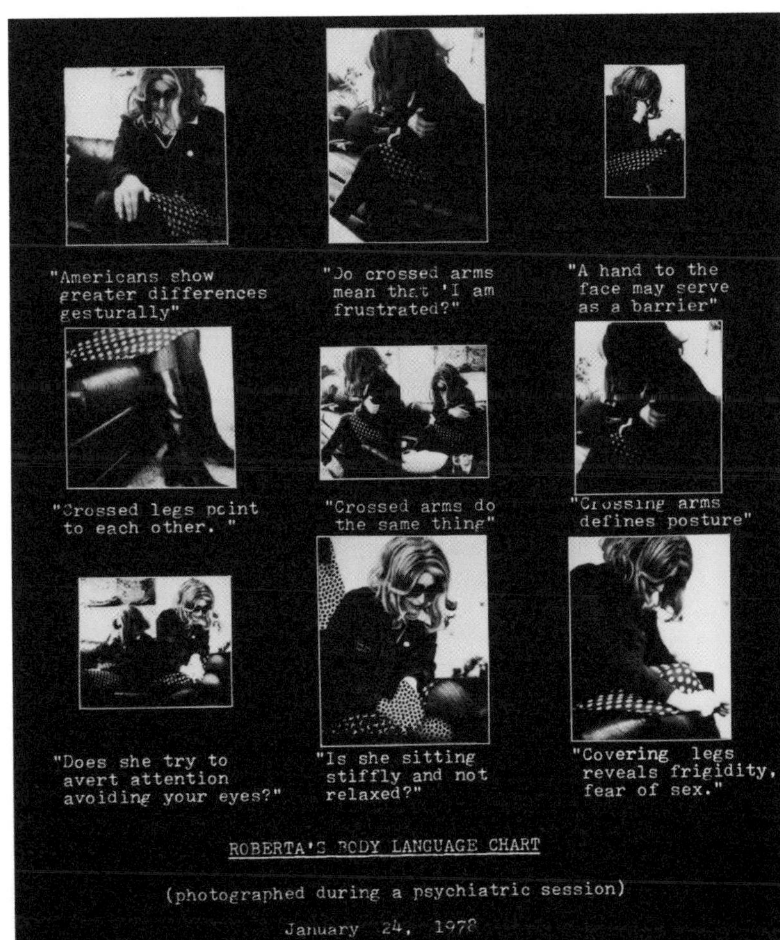

FIGURE 4
Lynn Hershman Leeson, *Roberta's Body Language Chart*, 1978/2009. Gelatin silver print; 40 1/2 × 33 1/2 in. (102.9 × 85.1 cm). Tate, Presented anonymously 2010.

the edge of reality, and how you tell truth from fiction.

After all, if you have a fictional person who's using all of living reality as a description of what her life is like, you have someone who's reflecting the world around her. I've restaged a few pieces of Roberta's *evidence* through that lens, but they become just a historical reference for what happened during that point in culture.

WB I have to say, I arrived at a very different understanding of performance. Back when I first arrived in the States, I was disenchanted by the plastic arts, and I didn't see how such works could create empathy. I think that was because of the political or cultural disconnect I felt between the viewer and my subjects. So, when I started using my body in performance, it created the very thing I was looking for, which is empathy, and once you create empathy for your subject, you start creating a dialogue. I think that's when I arrived at the idea that the body has its own language, and I think that performance becomes the medium to explore that language. You are staging these encounters between the body, performance, and technology, and in doing so you are creating a pathway to a very powerful connection. But I agree with Lynn—it's difficult to repeat these performances because they are tied to time and place.

BK The fact that you both touched on performance as being so linked to specific moments in time made me think about how you've both given audiences twenty-four-hour access to your bodies. First, I'm curious why constant observation was important to those projects, and second, I'm curious about the function of the audiences' anonymity that accompanies these projects.

WB Anonymity. I love that word because it's both powerful and dangerous. It is powerful because it allows people to act on their impulses, but that also represents the danger of it. Regarding twenty-four hours, that notion came to me as I was performing *Domestic Tension*. On the first day of that performance, Susan Aurinko at FlatFile [Gallery] said to me, "So, we should go home now. It's five o'clock." And I responded, "Susan, Iraqis in a war zone don't go home at five o'clock. They don't close down shop like, 'all right, we are done for today.'" This was political art, and for political art to be active, it has to mirror life, which meant putting my body in front of the camera, in front of people, and giving them access twenty-four hours a day for an entire month.

Similarly, with the project *3rdi* (2010–11; pp. 64–75), it was about the constant nature of surveillance and living life as a Middle Eastern man in the US. People needed to see into my life for twenty-four hours a day, and I needed to return that gaze, in order for the work to feel true. So, it depends on the project and the project objective.

LHL I do a lot of work where the audience has to confront their lack of anonymity in today's age. In a recent installation, *Shadow Stalker* (2018–21), visitors were asked to type in their email address, and a digital shadow of themselves, created from their online history [retrieved from internet databases], would then be projected for everybody to see. Very often they're really surprised by the work because a whole lot of who a person is comes through just from their email address.

WB Yeah, there is no anonymity anymore. That being said, it was a little different when we made *Domestic Tension* in 2007, we tried to give enough freedom and space for people to be anonymous because I think there is power in that kind of agency. We wanted them to feel free, free enough to really act on their impulses, uninhibited by social and political judgment. Because really, if you set up boundaries, it might prevent people from acting the way they wanted to act. It might prevent people from showing you who they truly are.

BK I would like to end by asking a question I should've asked at the start, which is how do you two know each other? When did you meet?

WB God, it was 2010, I believe. I had recently finished the project *and Counting . . .* (2010; fig. 5), and that morning I took a plane to San Francisco to give a lecture at the Art Institute. That night, I had dinner with Lynn and a few other people, and after that, I crashed at the Fisherman's Wharf for three days because I was so sick and had so many fresh tattoos on my back that I couldn't move. Honestly, I didn't think I was going to make it to dinner because my back held all this pain, but by the time I got there, we had a beautiful conversation and I was able to pull through. I remember that far.

LHL That's amazing. You seemed normal.

WB Well, that was the performance, too.

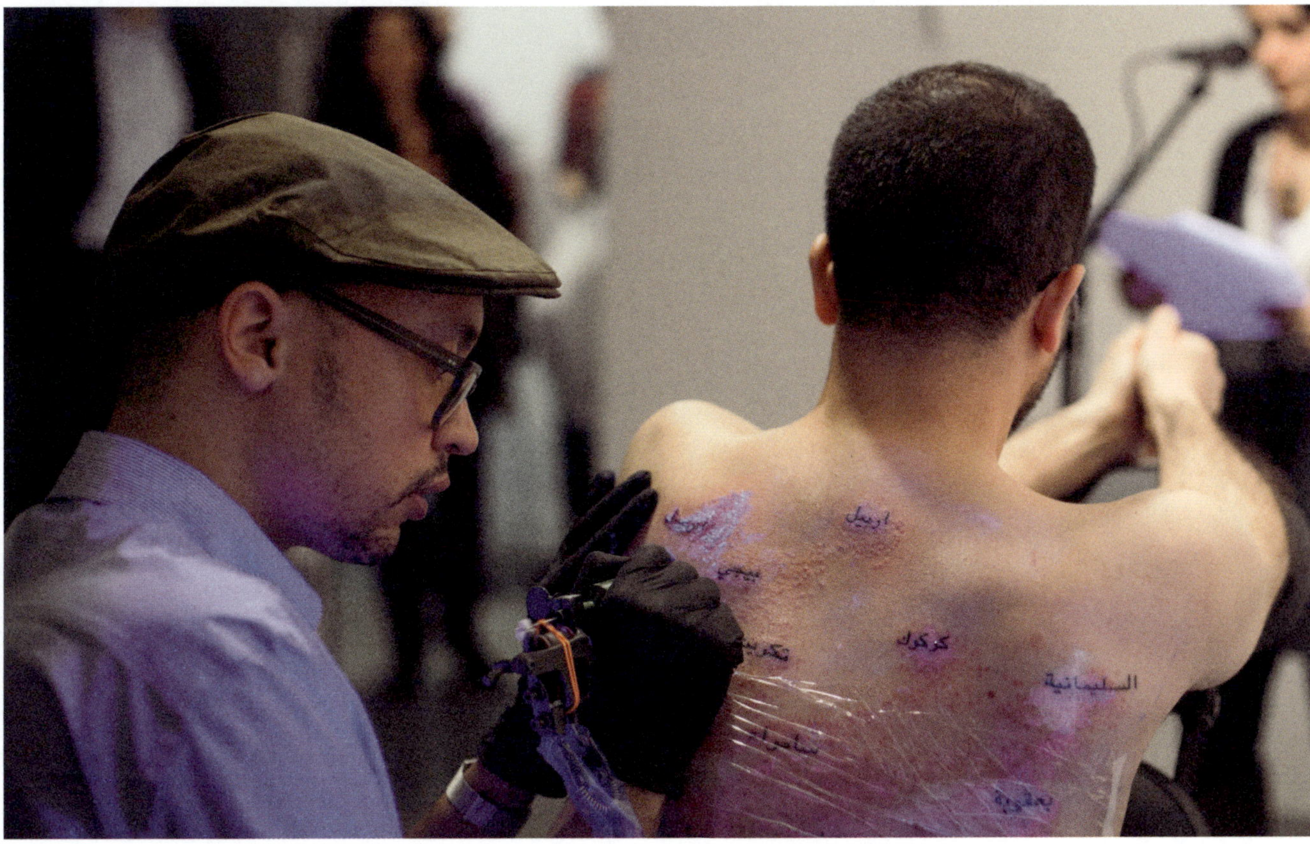

FIGURE 5
Wafaa Bilal, *and Counting . . .* , 2010.
Performance view: Elizabeth Foundation
for the Arts, March 8, 2010.

Images

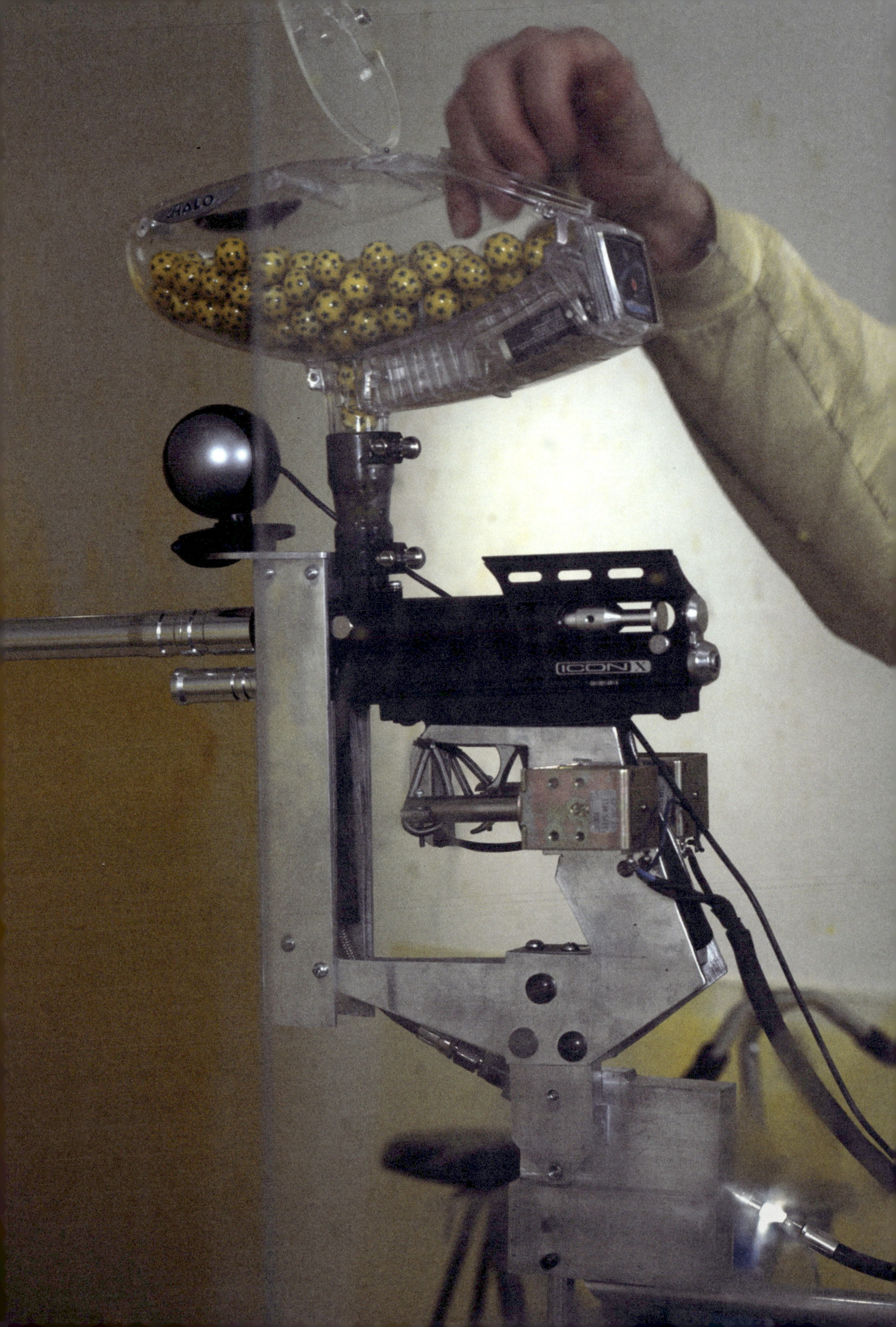
HALO
ICON X

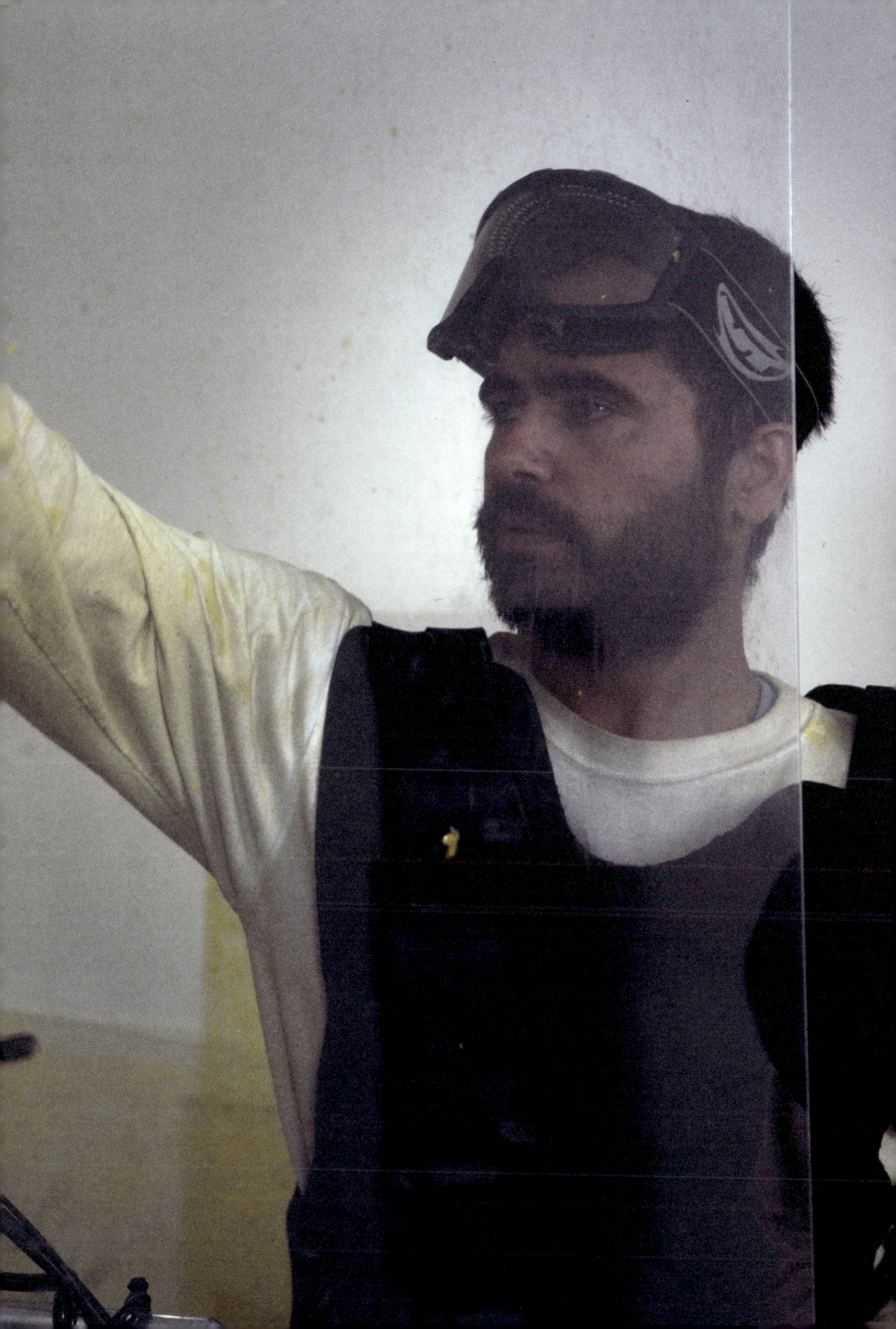

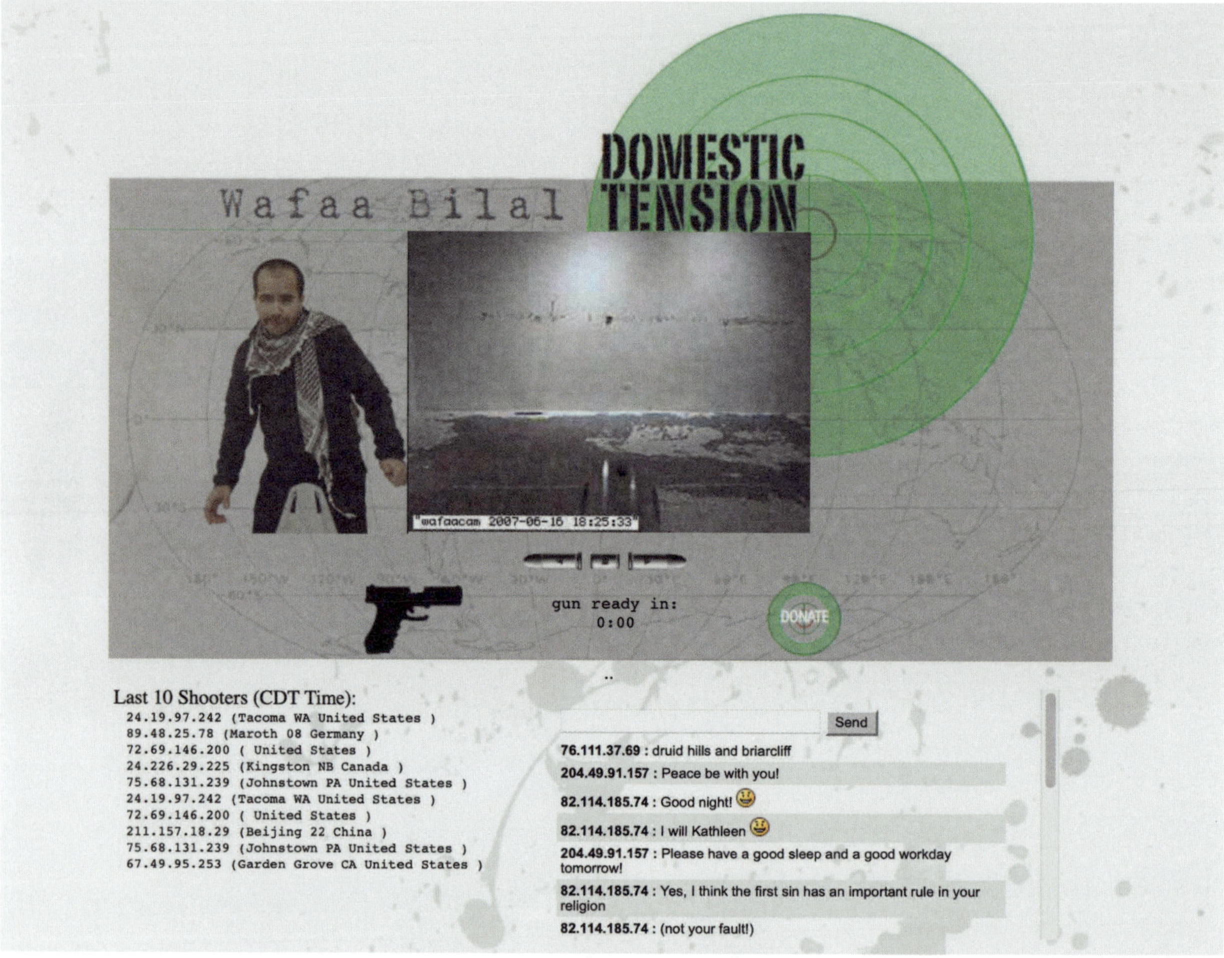

Wafaa Bilal
DOMESTIC TENSION
"wafaacam 2007-06-16 18:25:33"
gun ready in:
0:00
DONATE
Last 10 Shooters (CDT Time):
24.19.97.242 (Tacoma WA United States)
89.48.25.78 (Maroth 08 Germany)
72.69.146.200 (United States)
24.226.29.225 (Kingston NB Canada)
75.68.131.239 (Johnstown PA United States)
24.19.97.242 (Tacoma WA United States)
72.69.146.200 (United States)
211.157.18.29 (Beijing 22 China)
75.68.131.239 (Johnstown PA United States)
67.49.95.253 (Garden Grove CA United States)
Send
76.111.37.69 : druid hills and briarcliff
204.49.91.157 : Peace be with you!
82.114.185.74 : Good night!
82.114.185.74 : I will Kathleen
204.49.91.157 : Please have a good sleep and a good workday tomorrow!
82.114.185.74 : Yes, I think the first sin has an important rule in your religion
82.114.185.74 : (not your fault!)

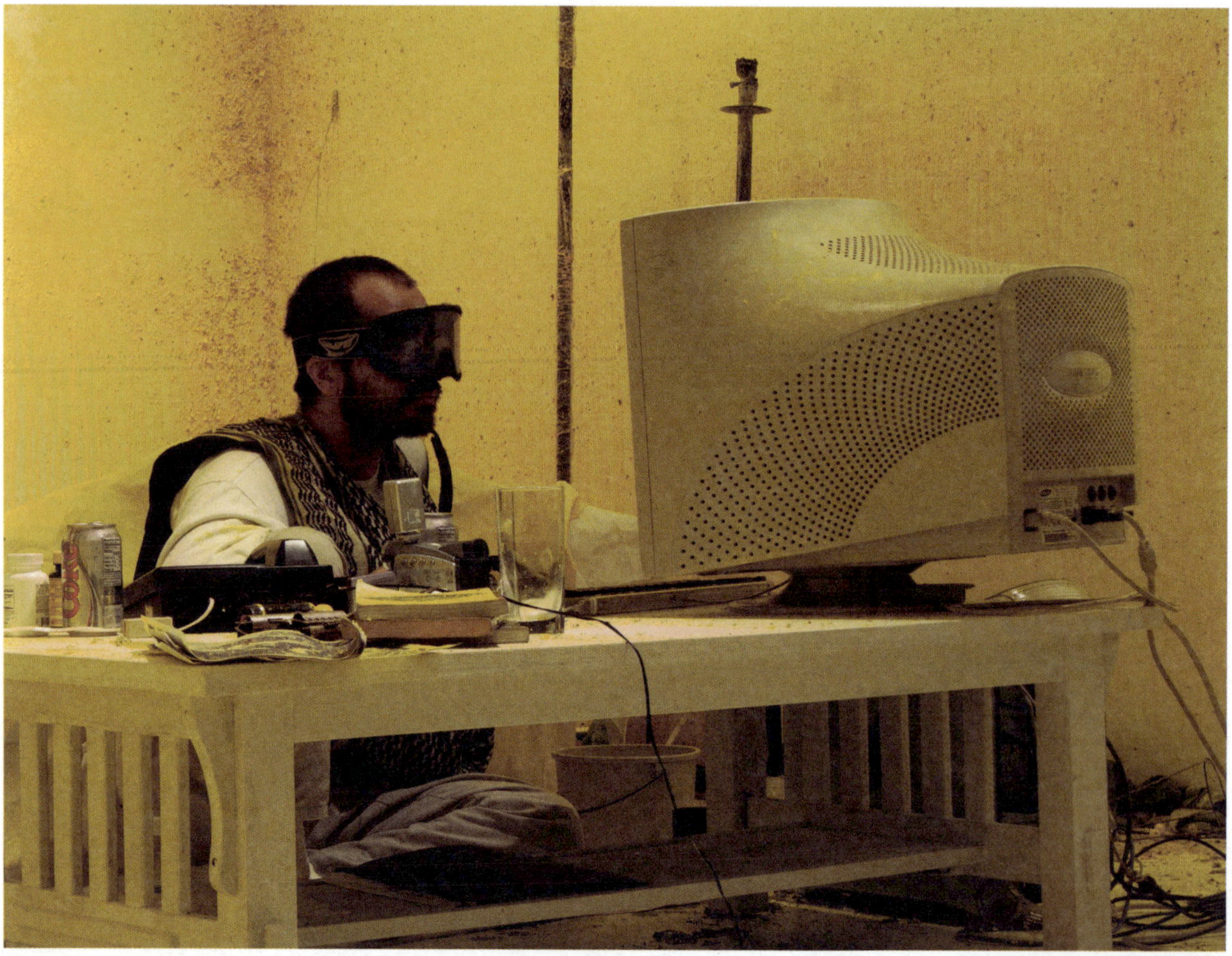

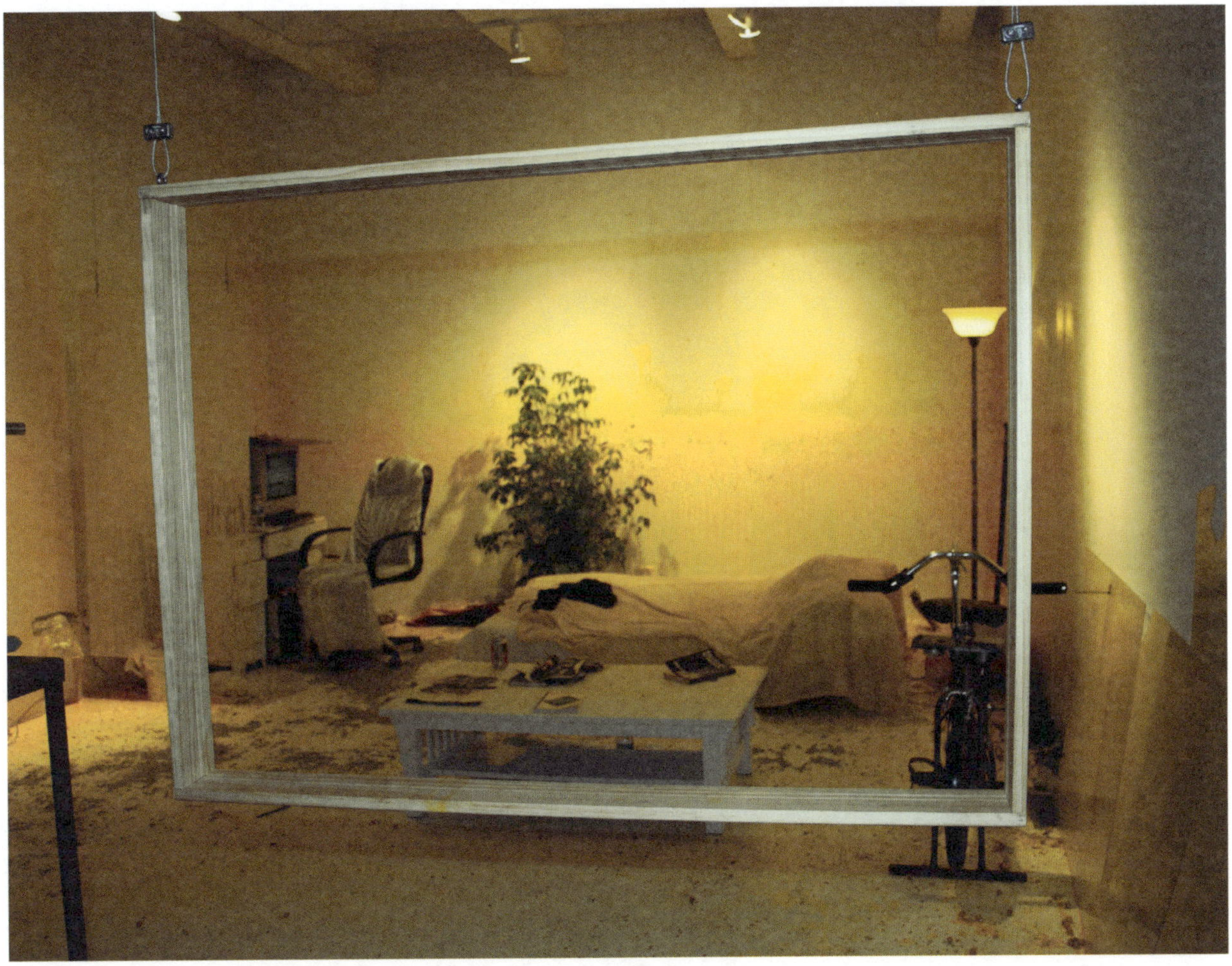

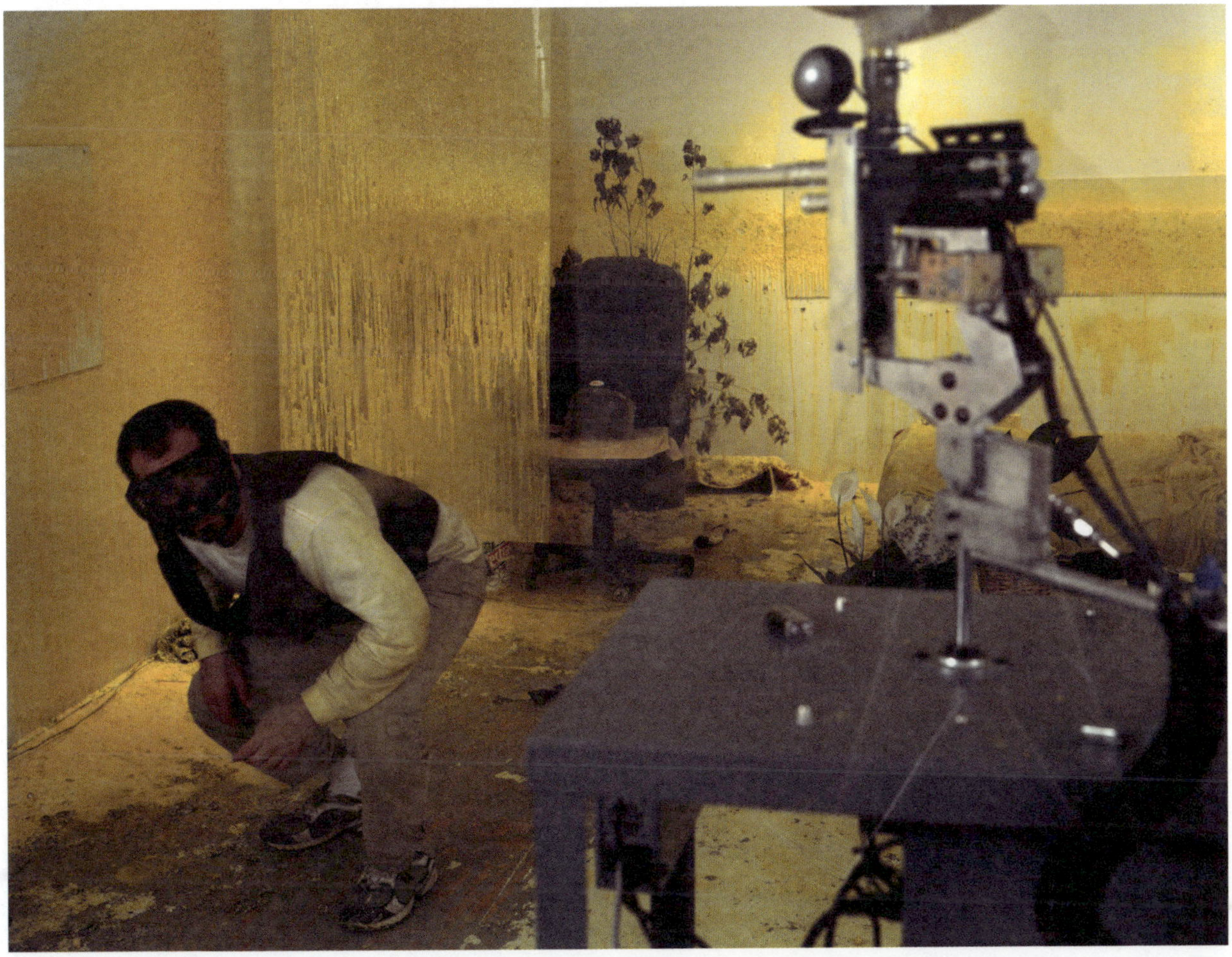

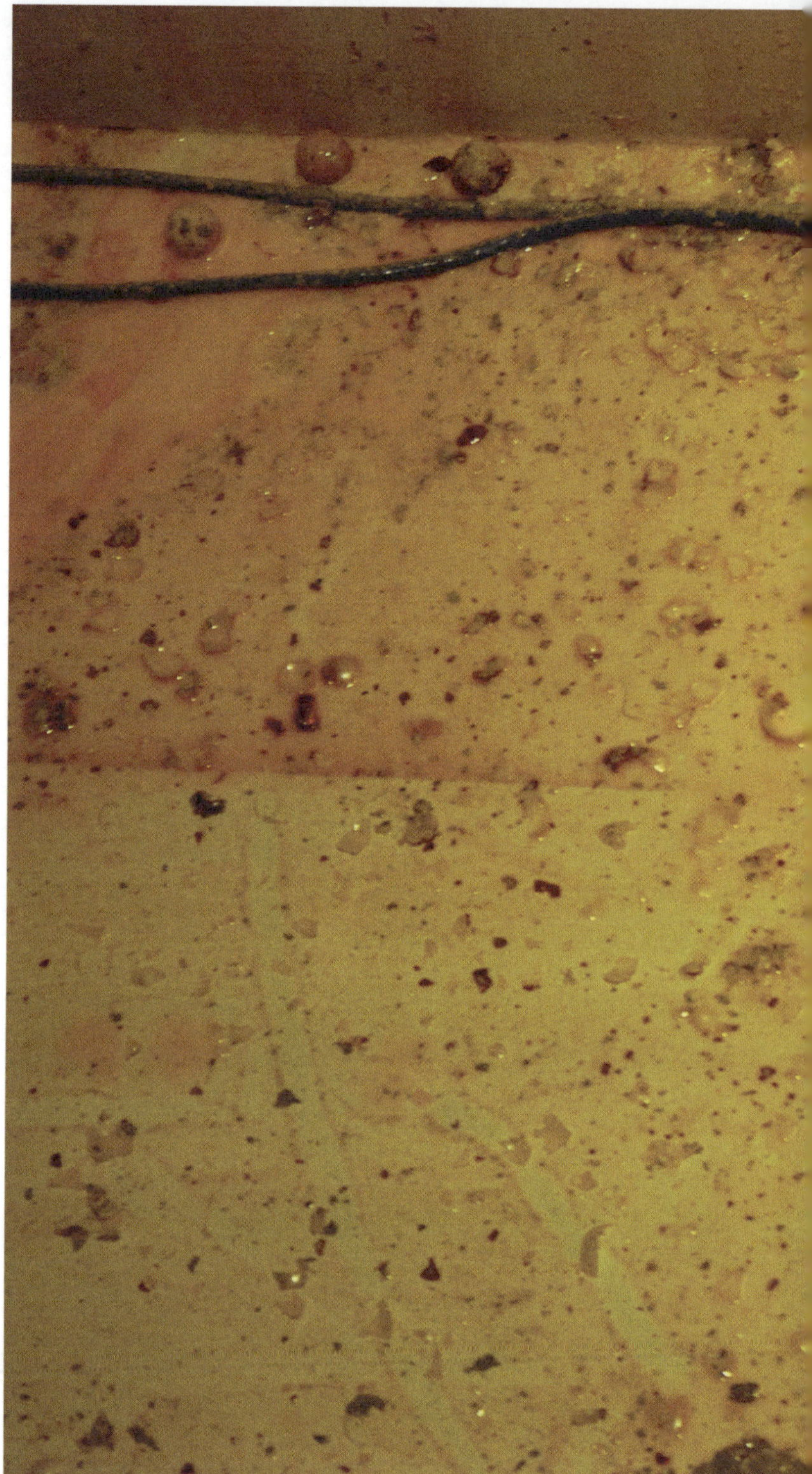

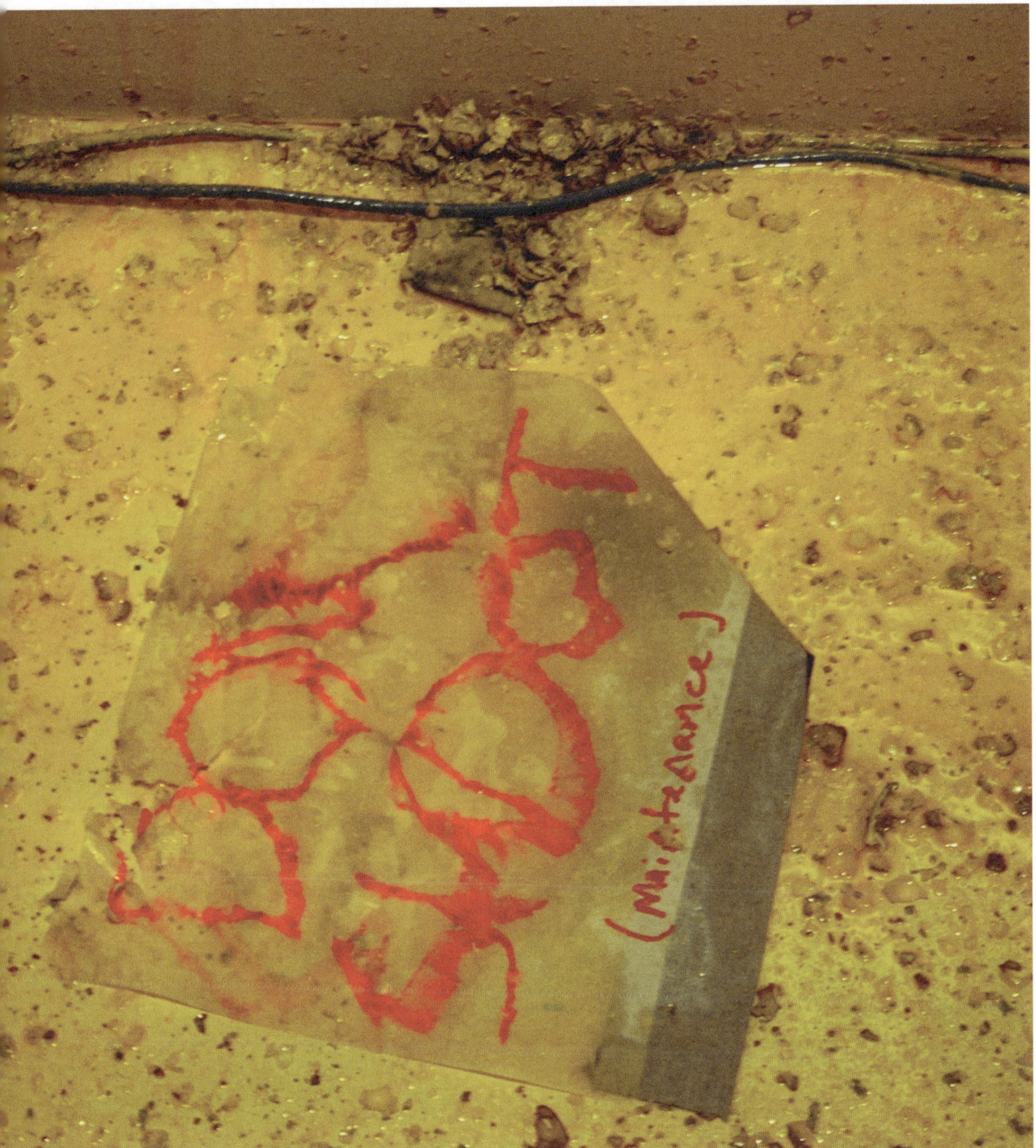
(Maintenance)

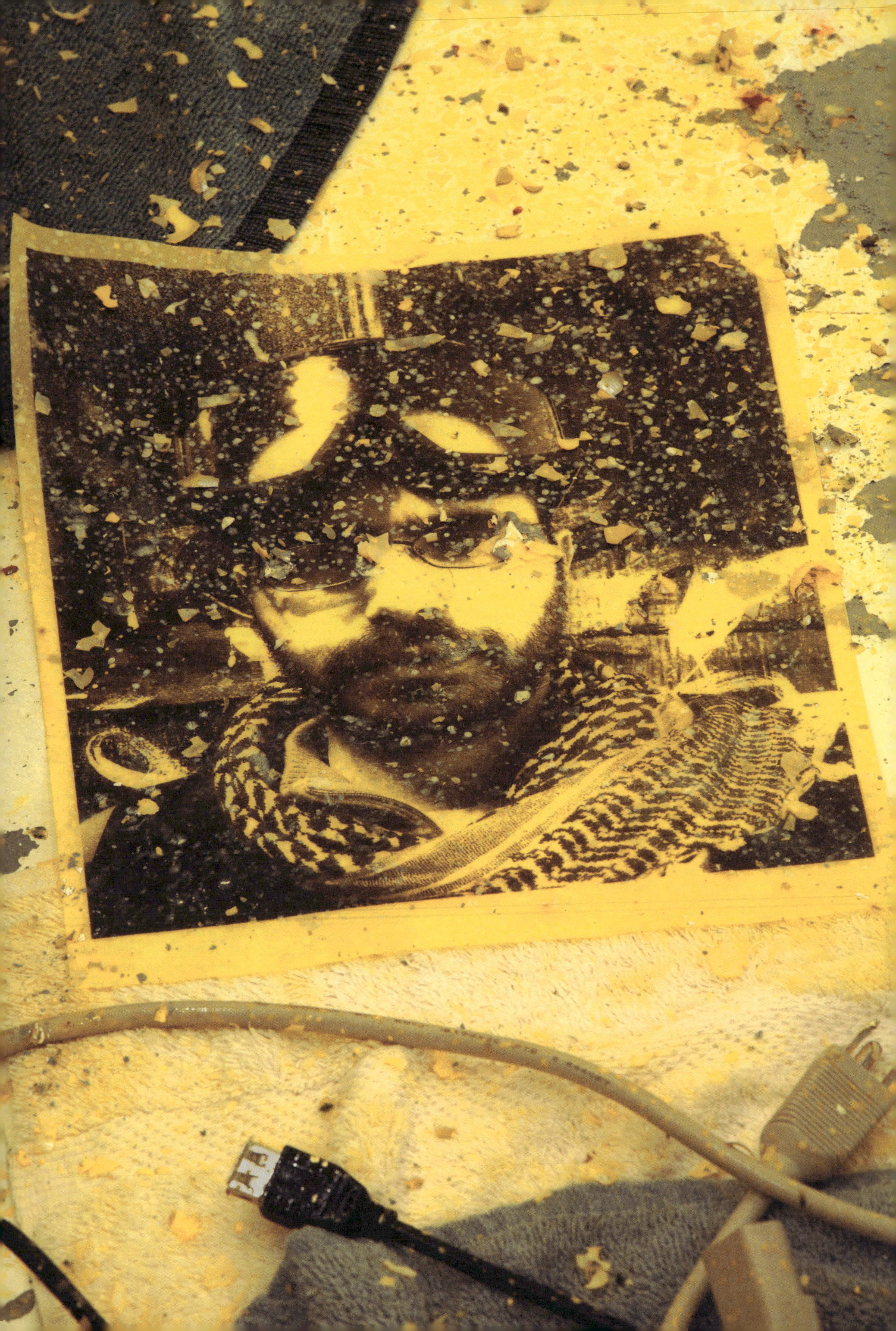

50–51	Wafaa Bilal refills the mounted, automated paintball gun, which he had to do regularly throughout his thirty-one-day performance at FlatFile Gallery in Chicago. Attached to the front of the gun is the webcam that was used to live stream the entirety of the performance.
52 (top)	The homepage for Bilal's *Domestic Tension* website. Visitors to the site could watch a live stream of the performance and interact with Bilal via live chat. They could also aim the paintball gun and fire it remotely, though when they did, their IP addresses would populate under a list of recent "shooters."
52 (bottom)	Bilal sits at his computer, where he interacted with participants through an online chat room hosted on the *Domestic Tension* website. Also pictured is a video camera Bilal used to document his daily experiences and a phone the gallery owner installed to regularly check in on the artist.
53 (top)	Installation view of the FlatFile Gallery space, which functioned as Bilal's bedroom for the entirety of *Domestic Tension*. In the foreground is a protective plexiglass frame, behind which Bilal could retreat. On the twentieth day of his performance, Bilal removed this plexiglass shield because it had become so coated with paint that viewers couldn't see through it.
53 (bottom)	Bilal ducks below the line of paintball fire. Notably, Bilal's original title for *Domestic Tension* was *Shoot an Iraqi*.
54–55	A sign reading "Don't Shoot (Maintenance)" lies in a pool of paintball residue. At times throughout the performance, Bilal had to repair the weapon that was shooting at him.
56	A photograph of Bilal lays on the ground, covered in yellow paint splatter.

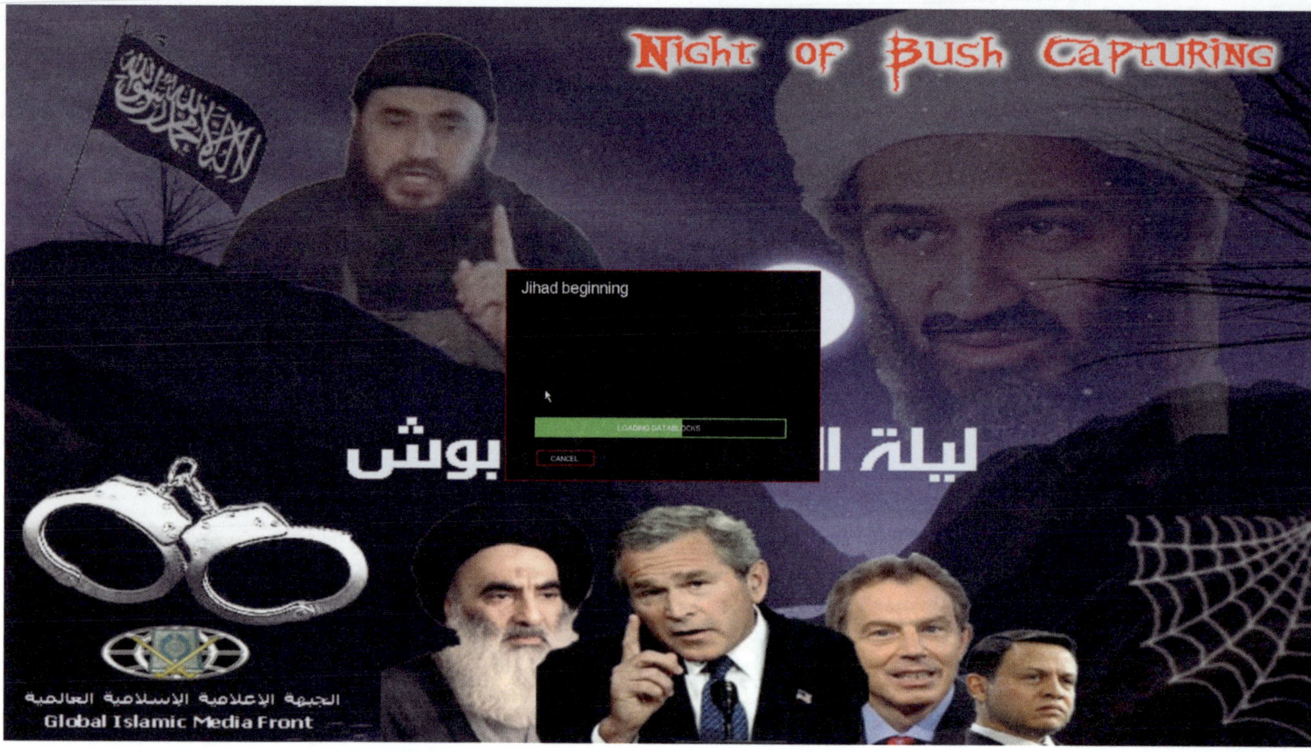
Night of Bush Capturing
Jihad beginning
LOADING DATABLOCKS
CANCEL
الجبهة الإعلامية الإسلامية العالمية
Global Islamic Media Front

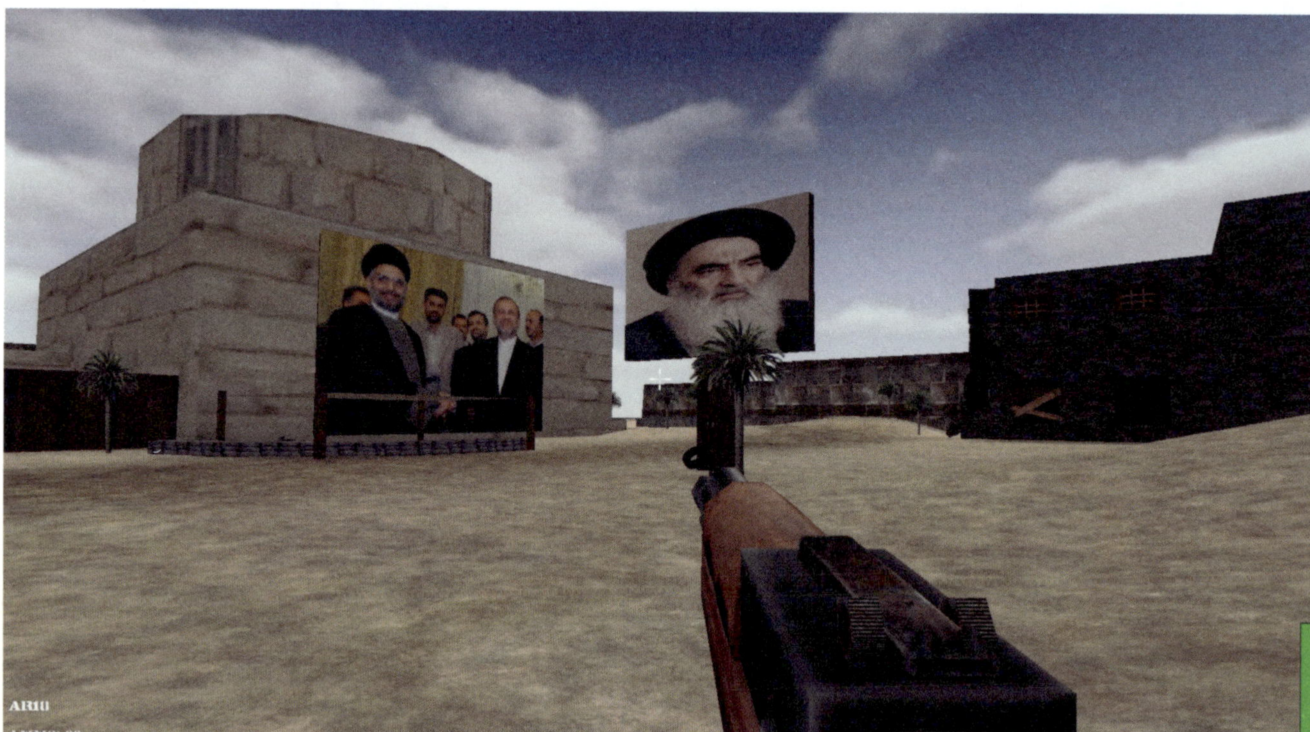
AR18
AMMO: 99

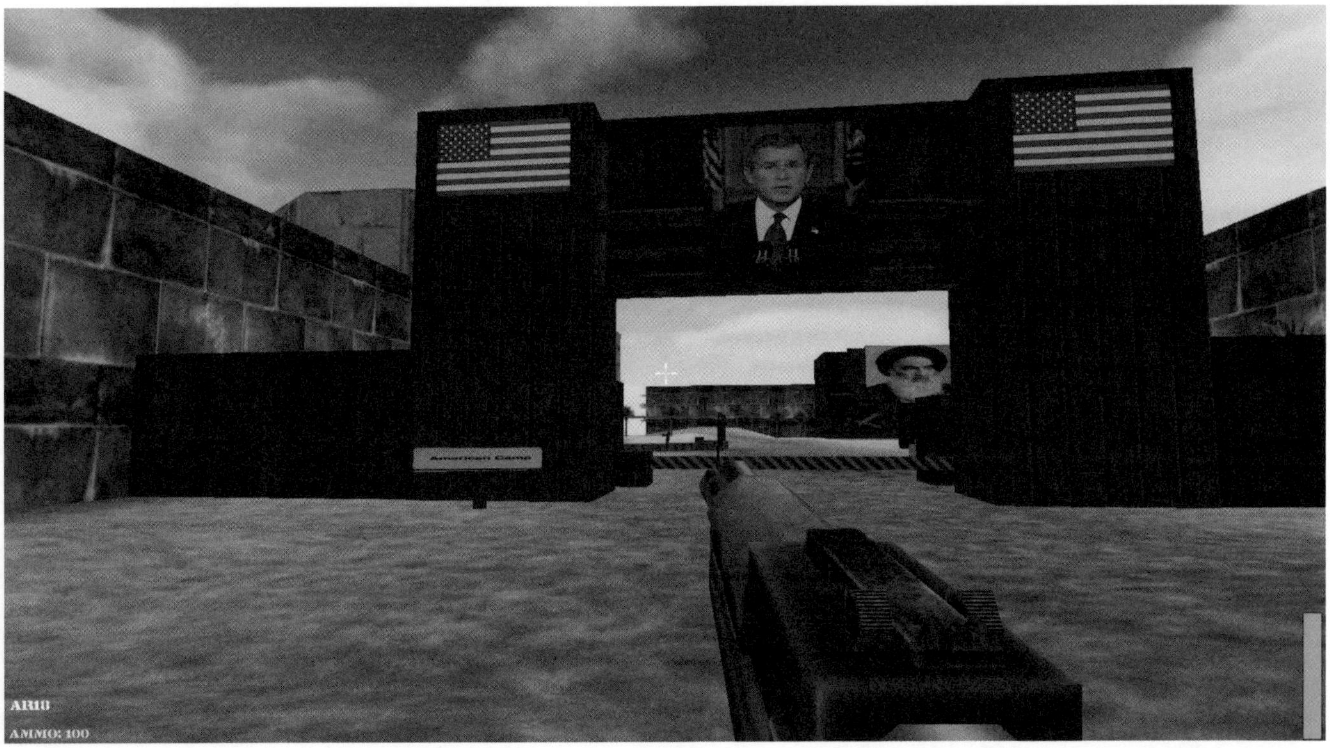
American Camp
AR18
AMMO: 100

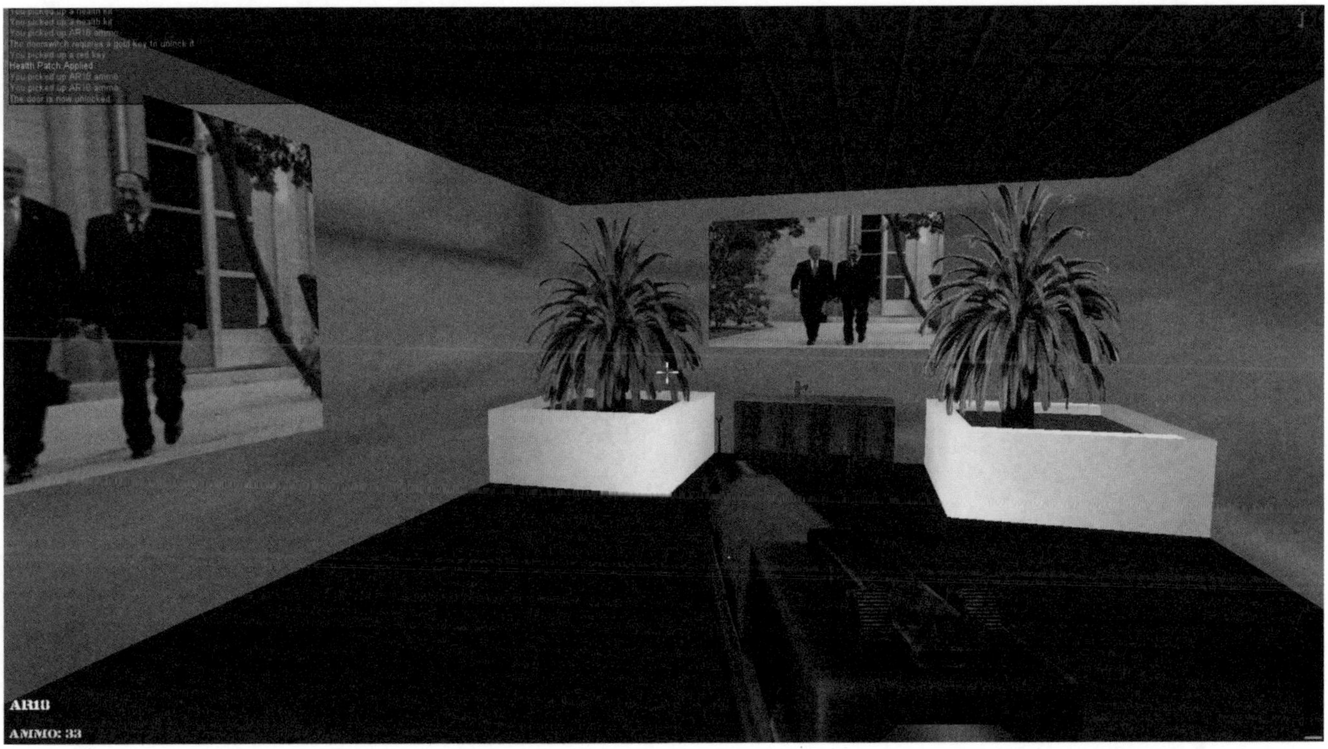
Health Patch Applied
AR18
AMMO: 33

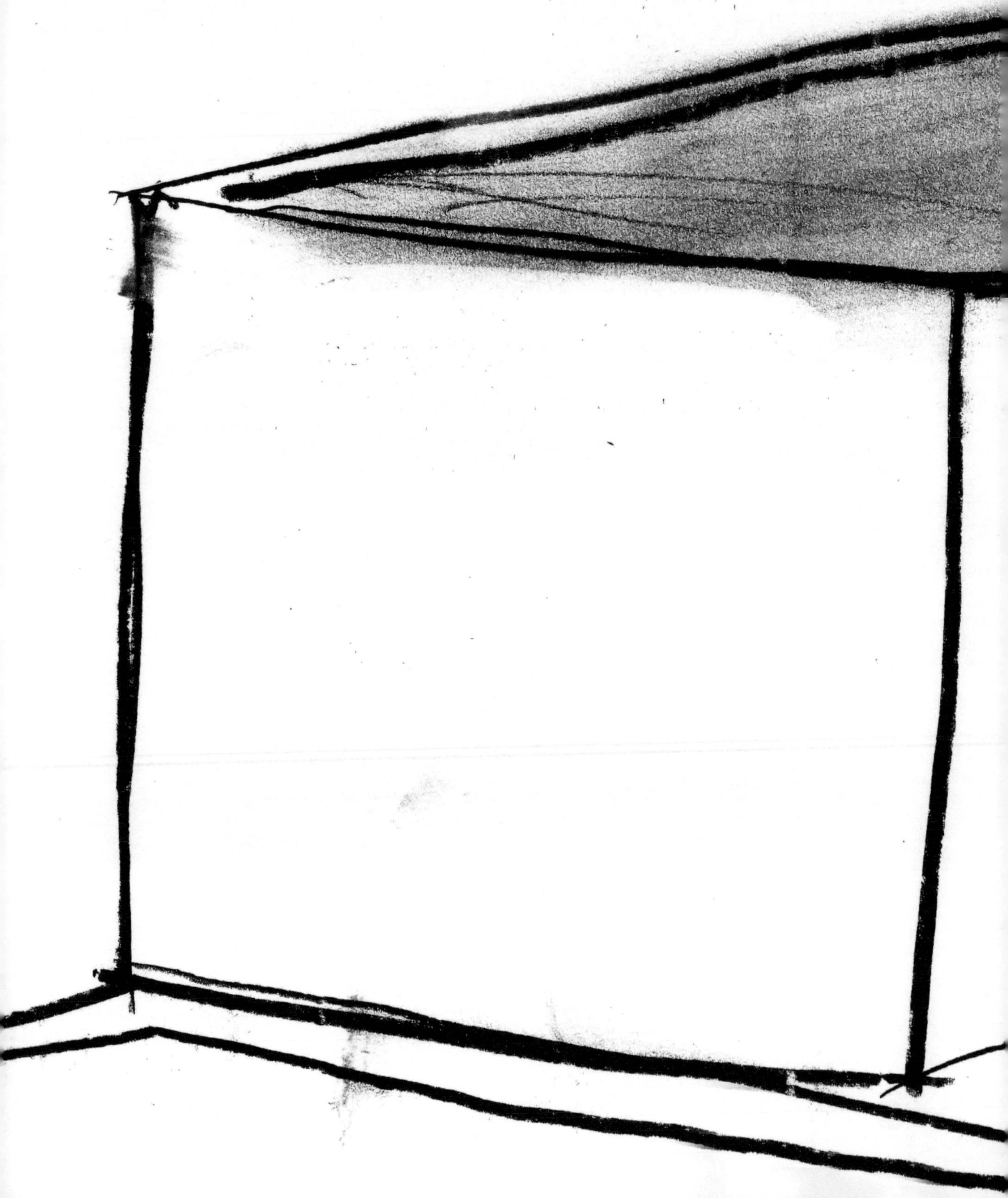

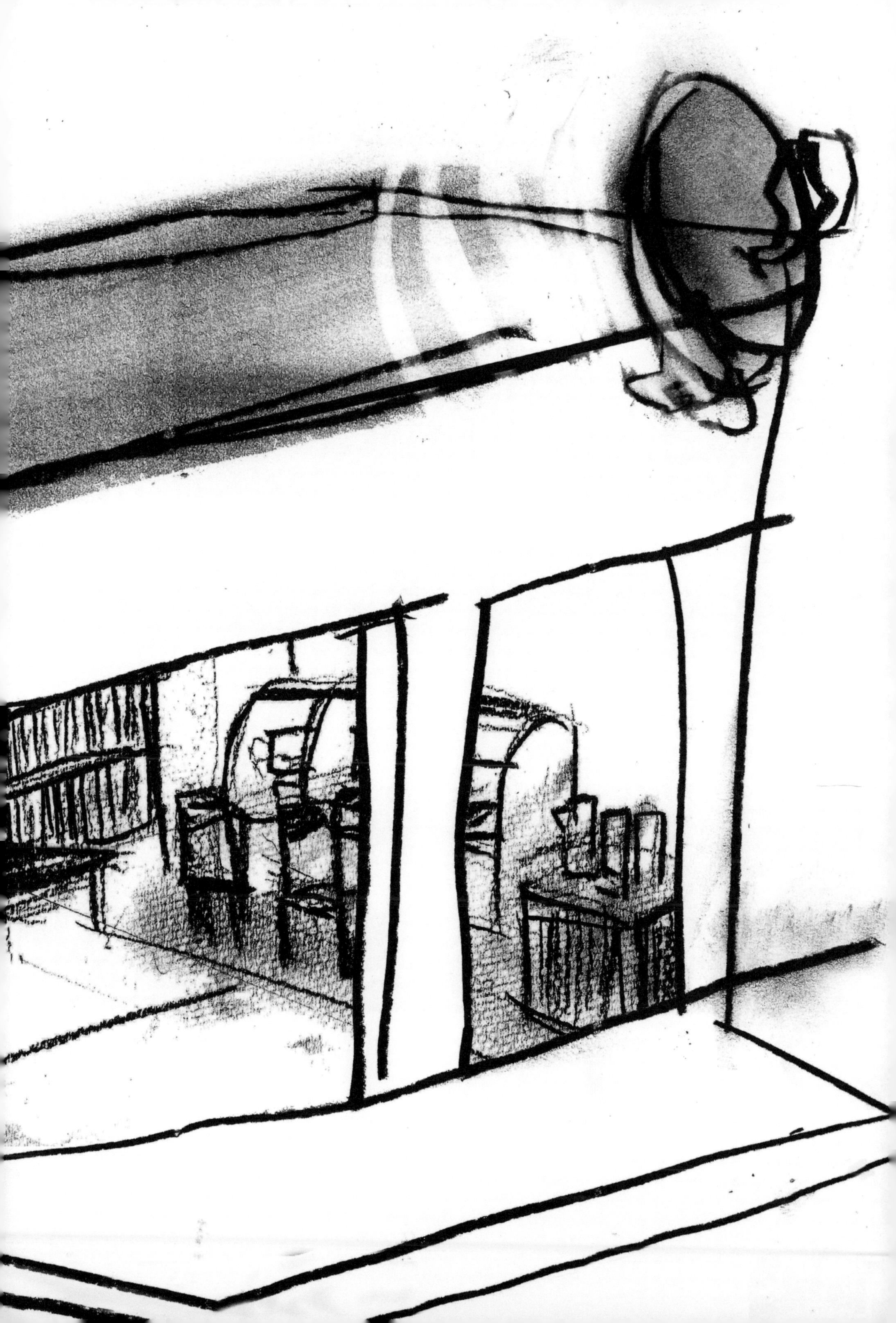

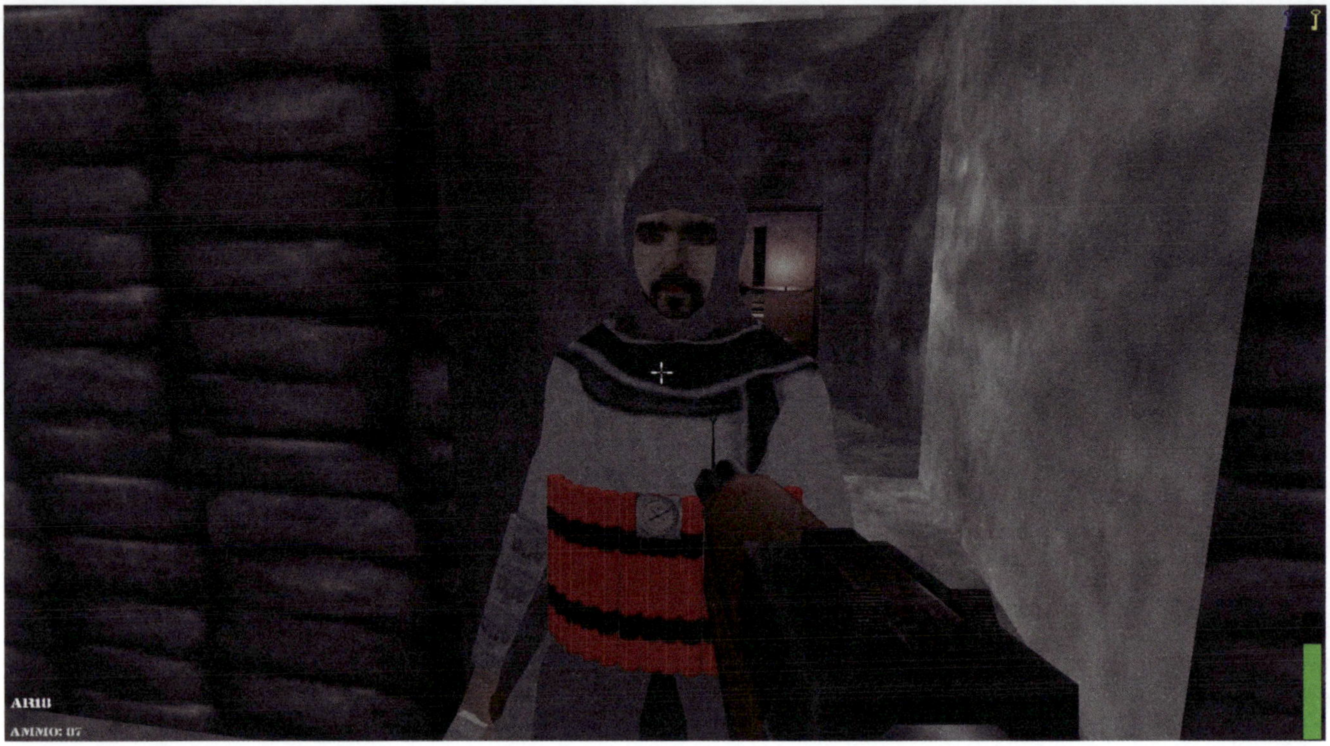
AR18
AMMO: 87

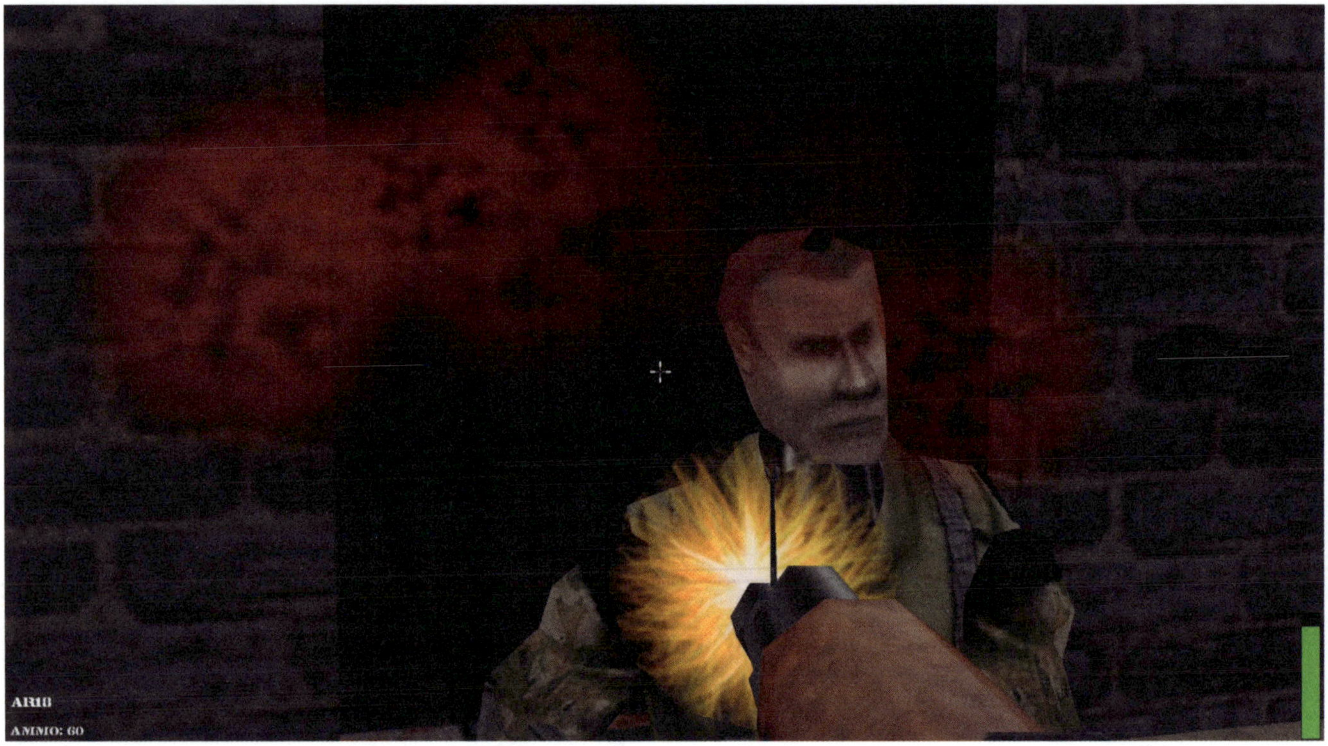
AR18
AMMO: 60

VIRTUAL JIHADI, 2008
VIDEO GAME

58 (top) — The title screen at the start of *Virtual Jihadi*, a first-person shooter video game. The image includes several political figures from the West, Central Asia, and the Arab world, such as former prime minister of the United Kingdom Tony Blair, former president of the United States George W. Bush, King Abdulla II bin Al-Hussein of the Hashemite Kingdom of Jordan, and Osama bin Laden.

58–59 — Various indoor and outdoor scenes from the point of view of the player in *Virtual Jihadi*. Since it is built atop two other versions of the game—an original called *Quest for Saddam* by a US-based amateur game developer and an al-Qaida–produced reskinning, *The Night of Bush Capturing*—players see a farrago of propaganda imagery as they navigate through each scene.

60–61 — A sketch of the internet café installation and gaming stations where visitors can play *Virtual Jihadi*, designed by Wafaa Bilal for the exhibition *Wafaa Bilal: Indulge Me* at MCA Chicago. The sketch was drawn by Bilal's longtime collaborator, James Kloiber.

62 (top) — The "virtual jihadi" character in Bilal's video game is a visual avatar of the artist himself. By casting himself as the game's suicide bomber, Bilal points to the expendability of the average Iraqi citizen.

62 (bottom) — The player shoots and hits a US solider. In the first version of the video game, *Quest for Saddam*, every soldier appeared with the face of Saddam Hussein. In the al-Qaida and Bilal versions, all the US soldiers are, likewise, identical.

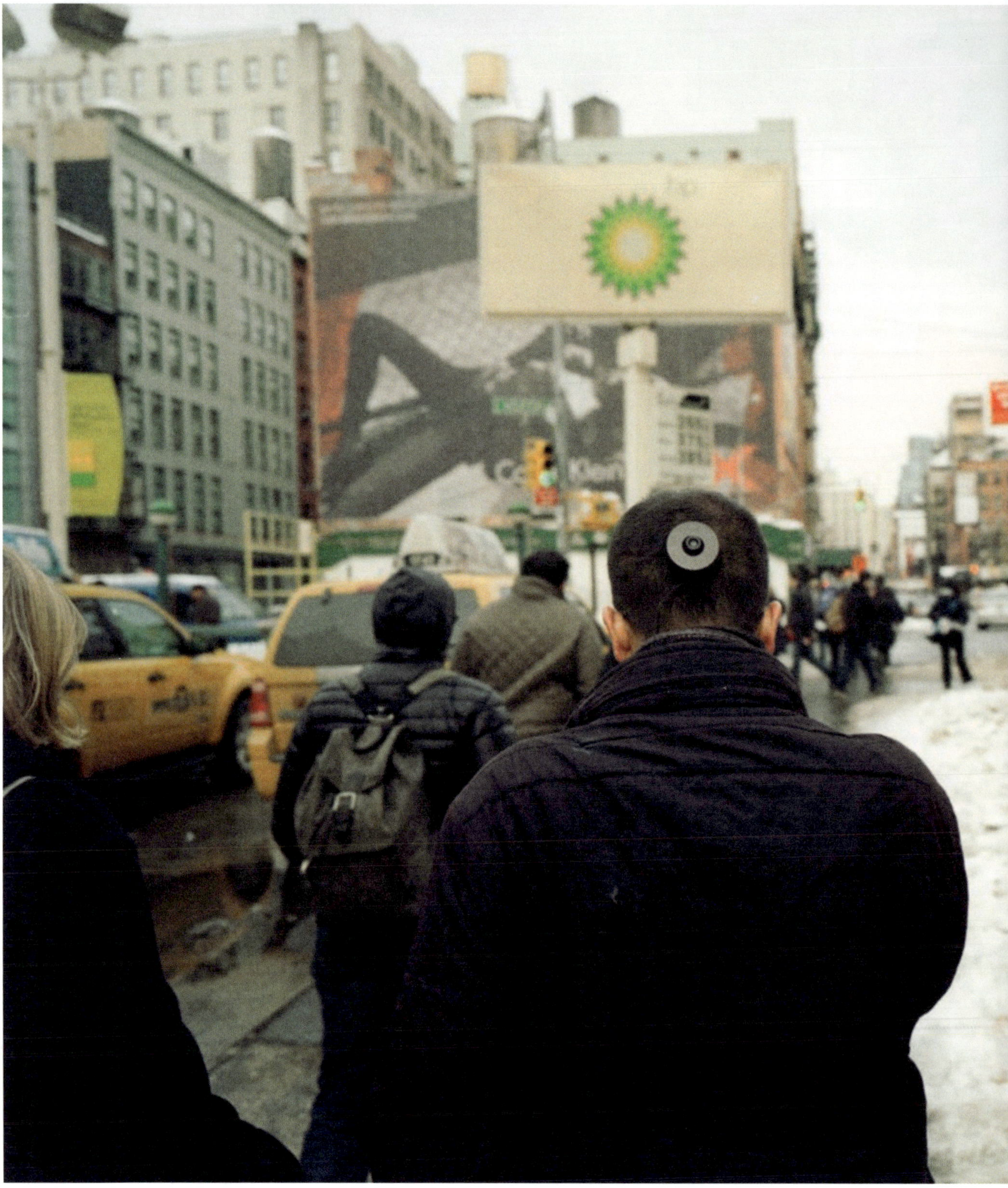

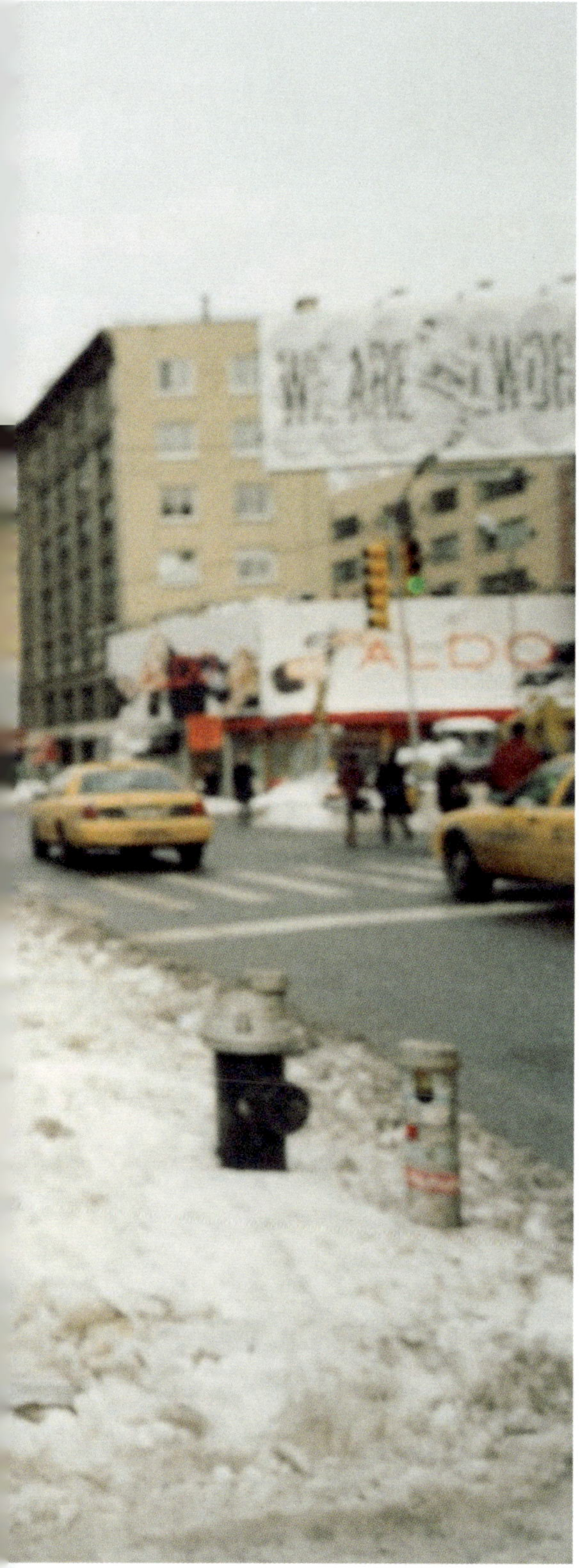
ALDO

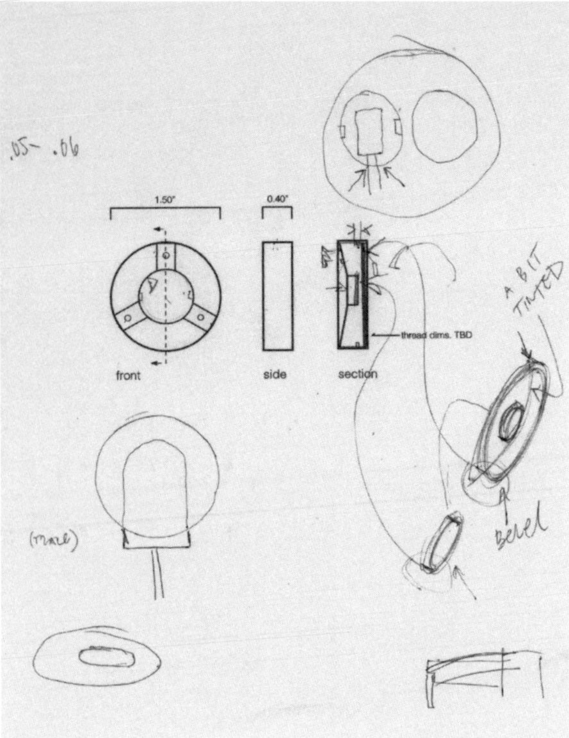
.05- .06
1.50"
0.40"
front
side
section
thread dims. TBD
A BIT TINTED
Bevel

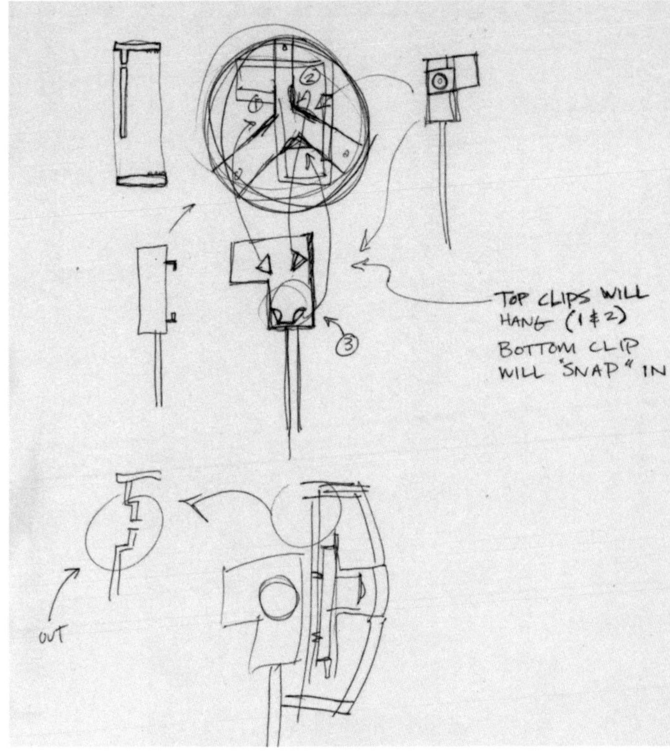
TOP CLIPS WILL HANG (1 & 2)
BOTTOM CLIP WILL "SNAP" IN
OUT

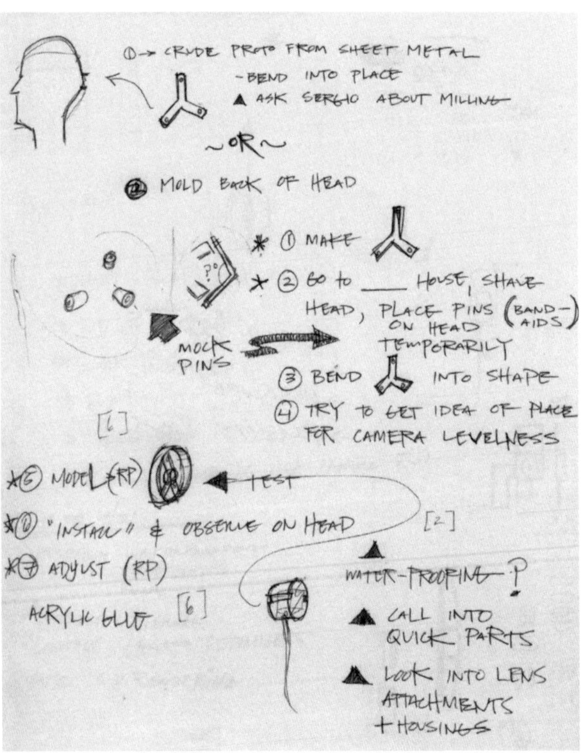
① → CRUDE PROTO FROM SHEET METAL
- BEND INTO PLACE
▲ ASK SERGIO ABOUT MILLING
~ OR ~
② MOLD BACK OF HEAD
* ① MAKE
* ② Go to ____ HOUSE, SHAVE HEAD, PLACE PINS ON HEAD TEMPORARILY (BAND-AIDS)
MOCK PINS
③ BEND INTO SHAPE
④ TRY TO GET IDEA OF PLACE FOR CAMERA LEVELNESS
*⑤ MODEL (RP)
TEST
*⑥ "INSTALL" & OBSERVE ON HEAD
*⑦ ADJUST (RP)
ACRYLIC GLUE
WATER-PROOFING ?
▲ CALL INTO QUICK PARTS
▲ LOOK INTO LENS ATTACHMENTS + HOUSINGS

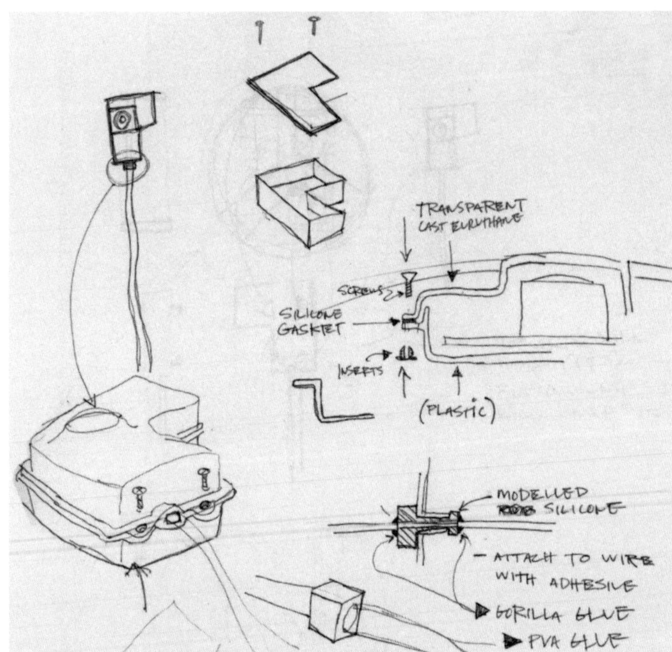
TRANSPARENT CAST EURETHANE
SCREWS
SILICONE GASKET
INSERTS
(PLASTIC)
MODELLED SILICONE
- ATTACH TO WIRE WITH ADHESIVE
GORILLA GLUE
PVA GLUE
"GOOP" PRODUCTS

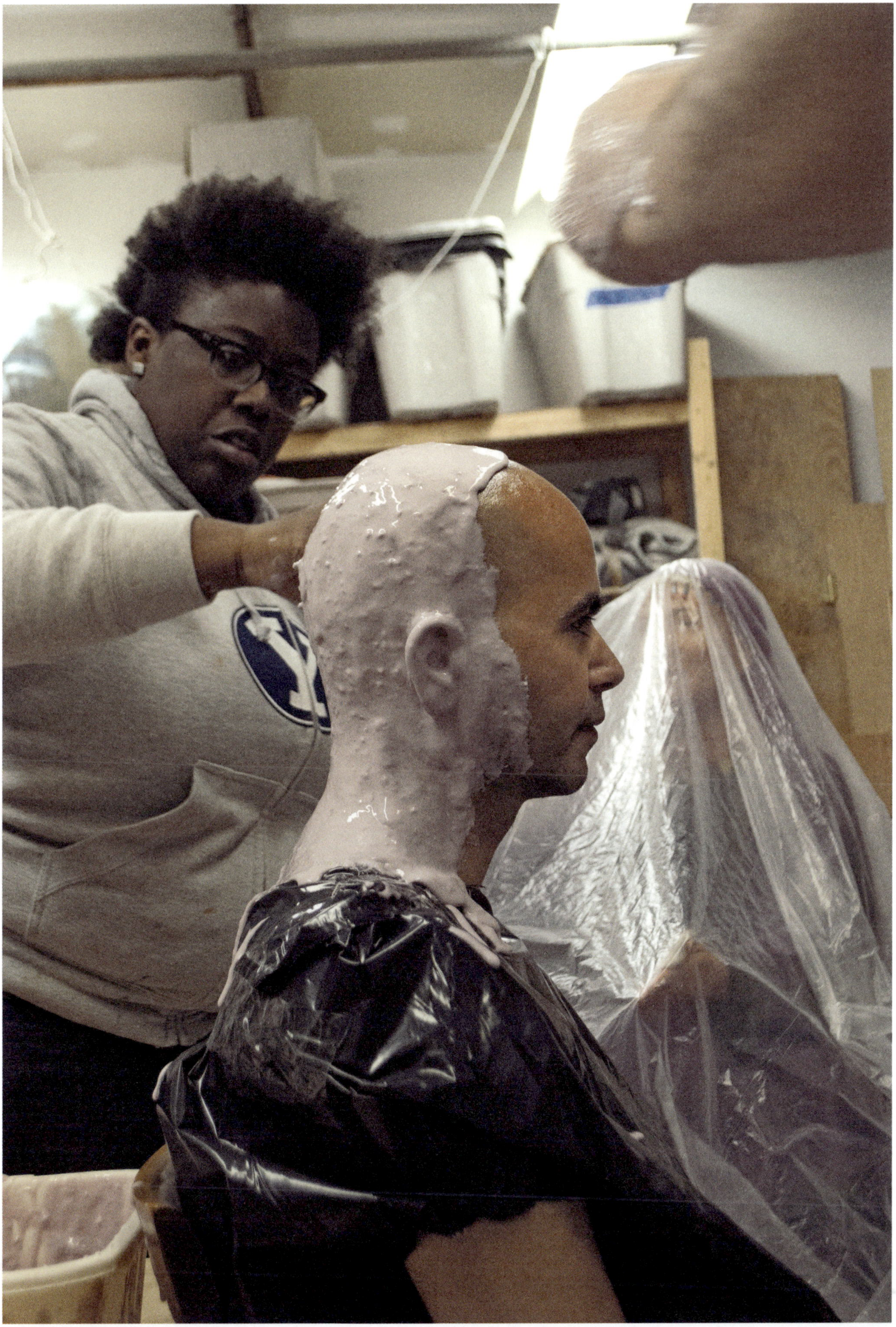

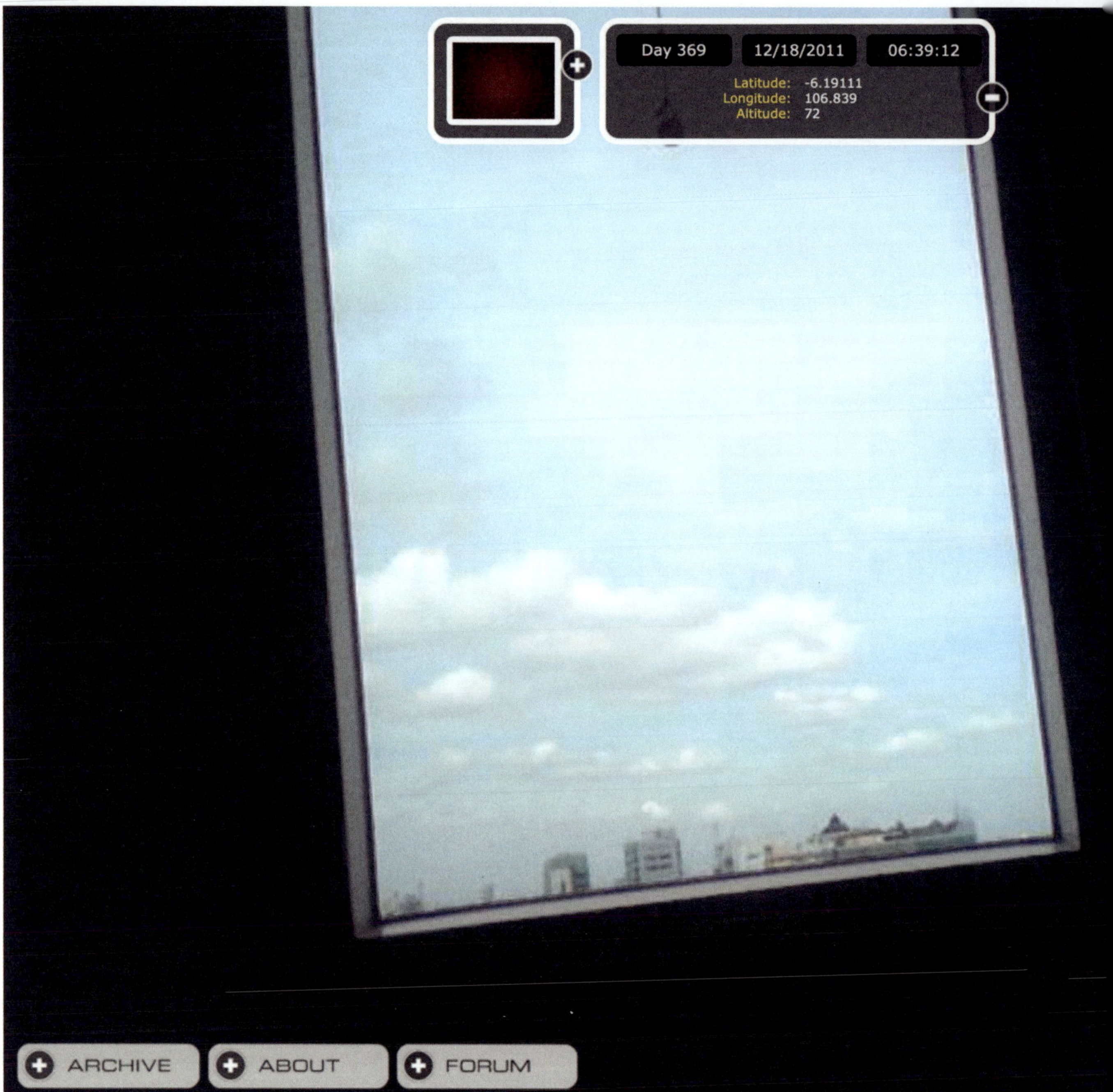
Day 369
12/18/2011
06:39:12
Latitude: -6.19111
Longitude: 106.839
Altitude: 72
ARCHIVE
ABOUT
FORUM

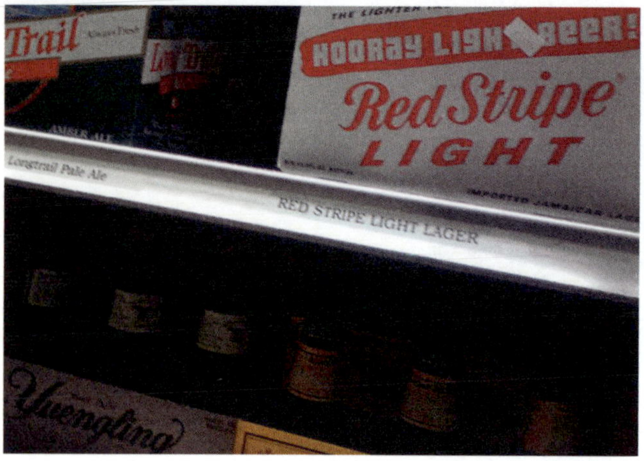
Trail
Red Stripe
LIGHT
Longtrail Pale Ale
RED STRIPE LIGHT LAGER
Yuengling

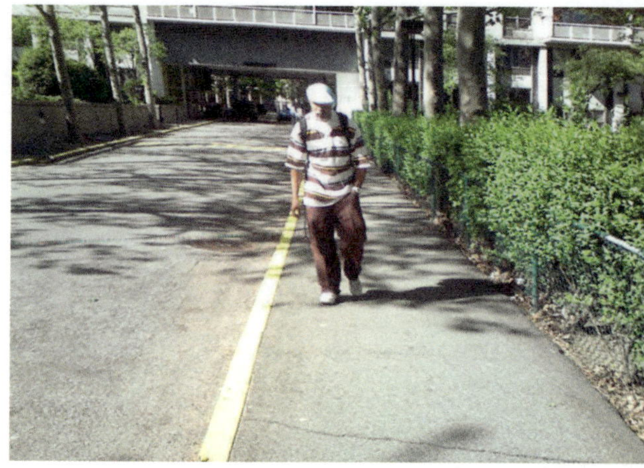

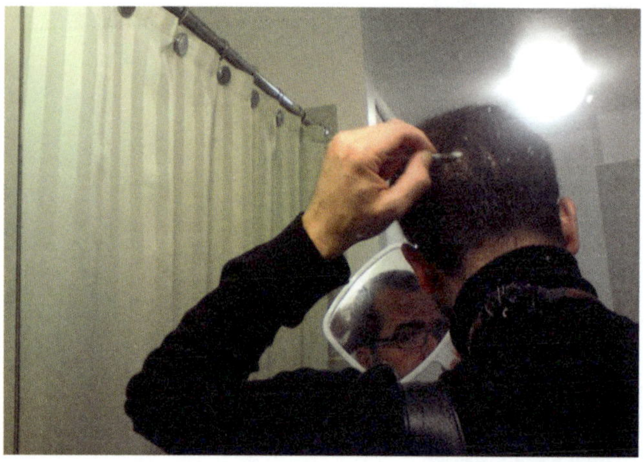

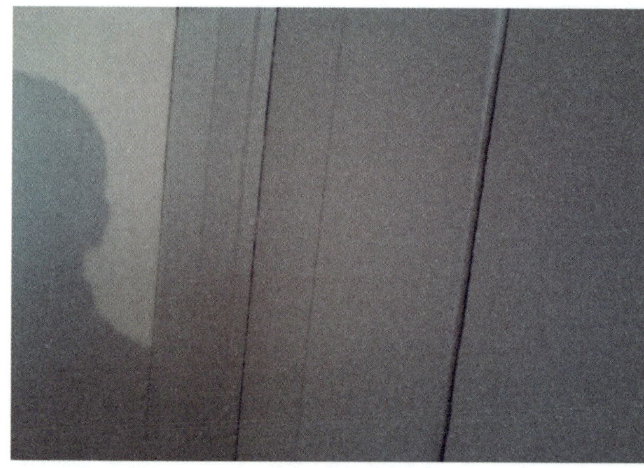

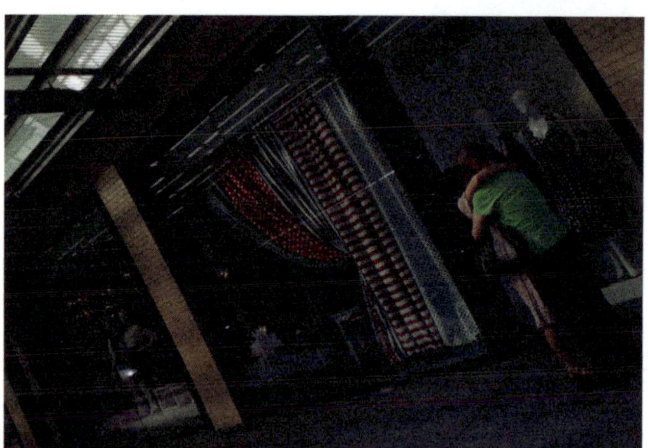

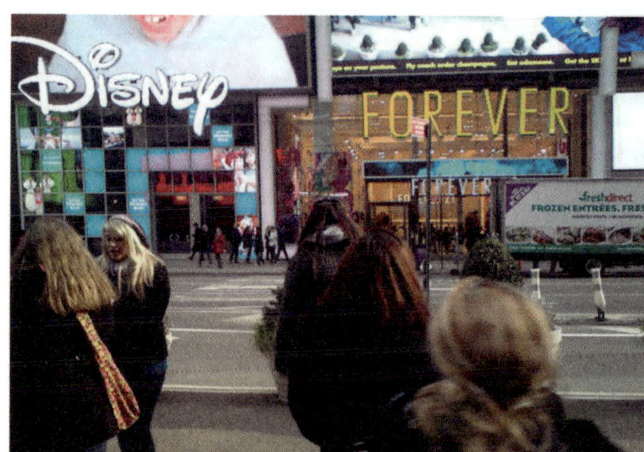
Disney
FOREVER
FOREVER
freshdirect
FROZEN ENTREES. FRESH

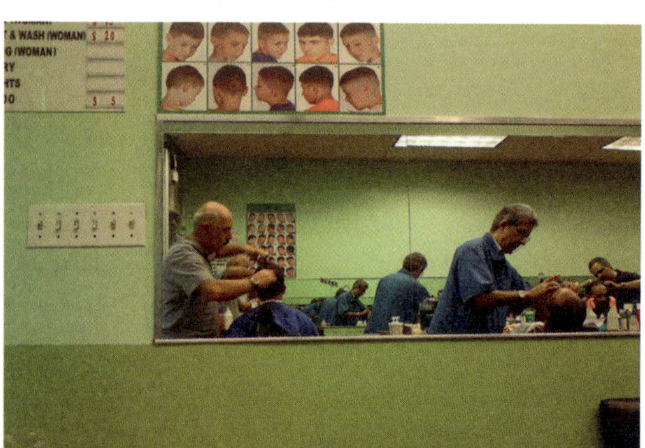

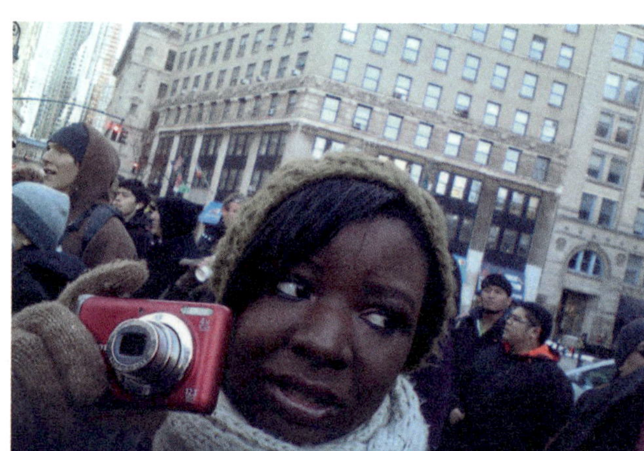

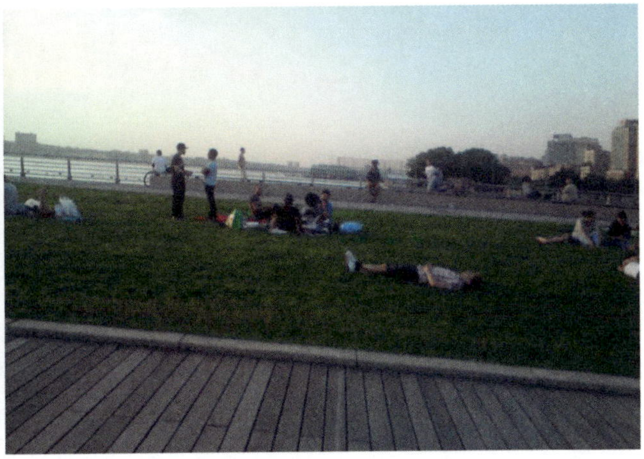

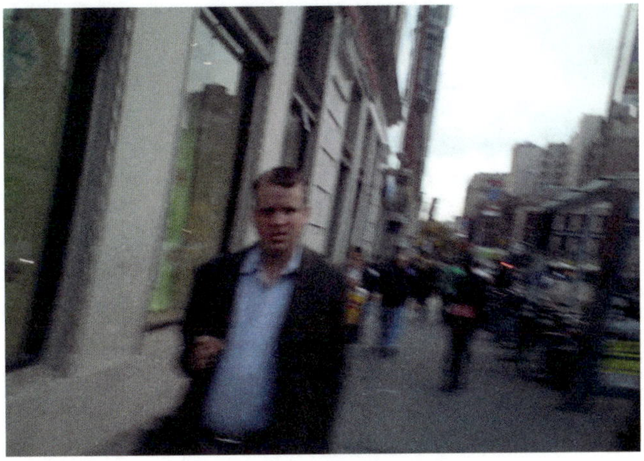

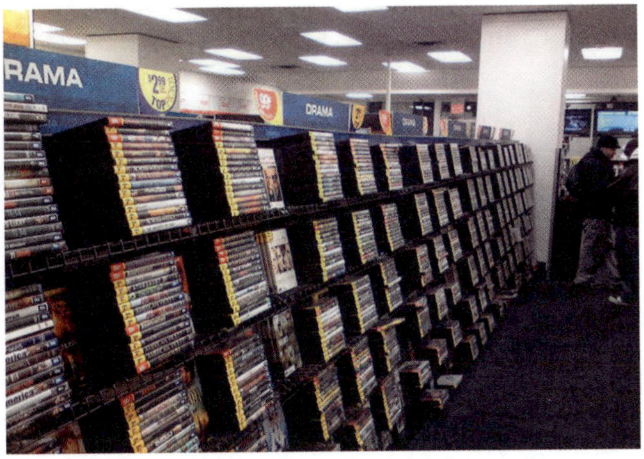
RAMA
DRAMA

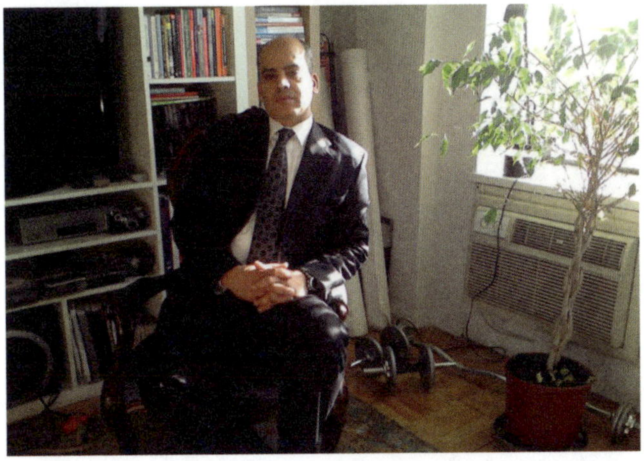

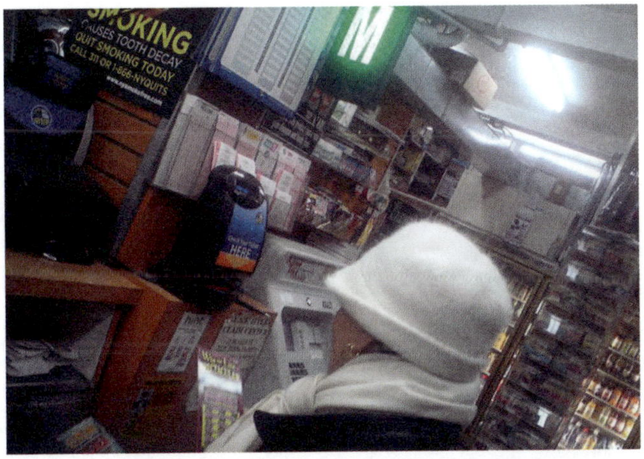
SMOKING
CAUSES TOOTH DECAY
QUIT SMOKING TODAY
M

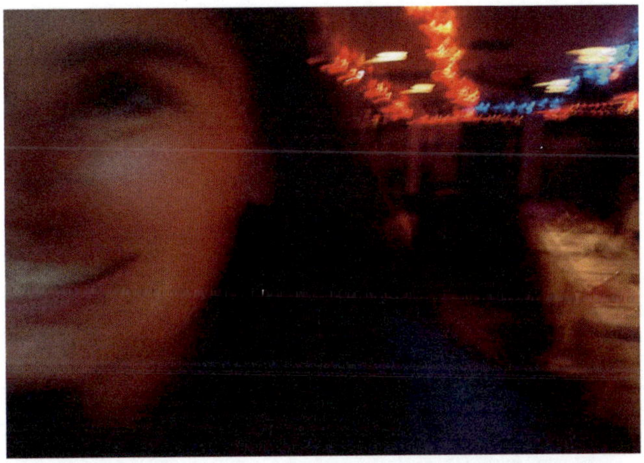

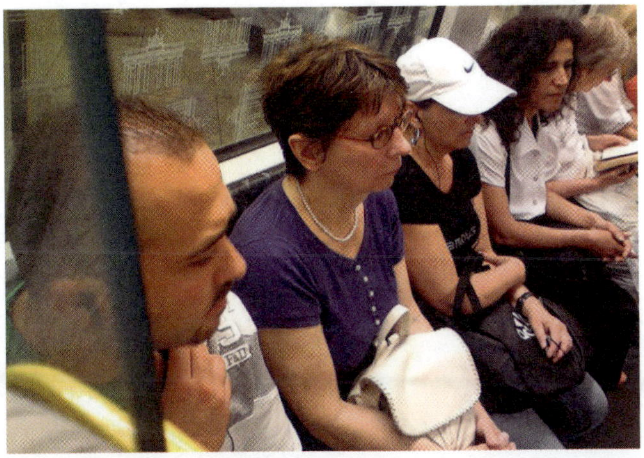

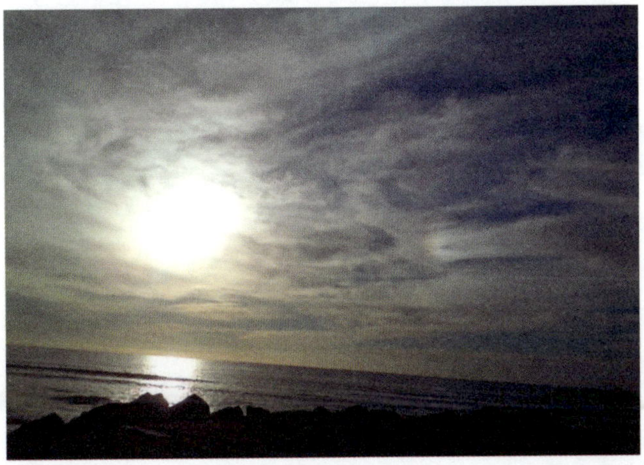

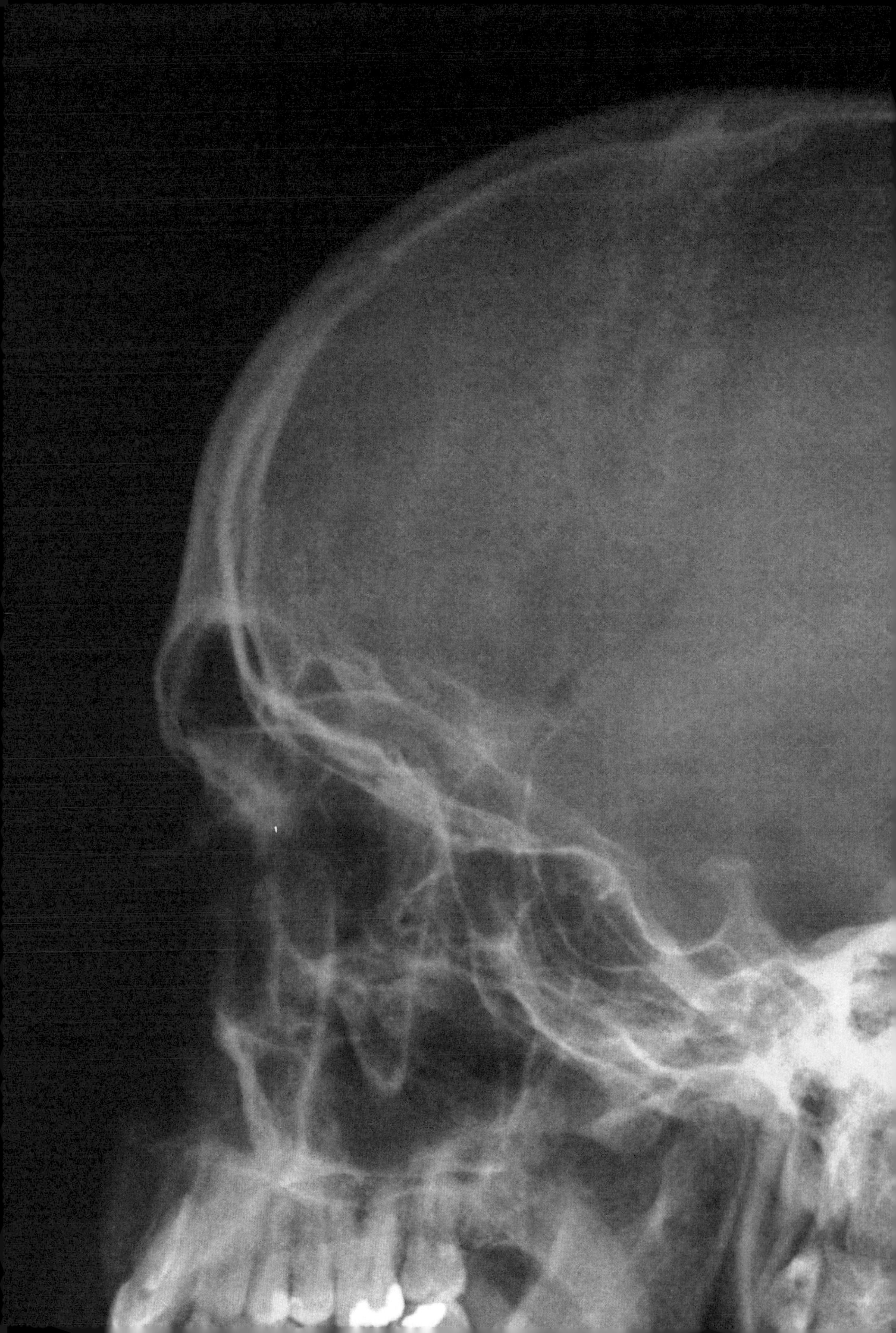

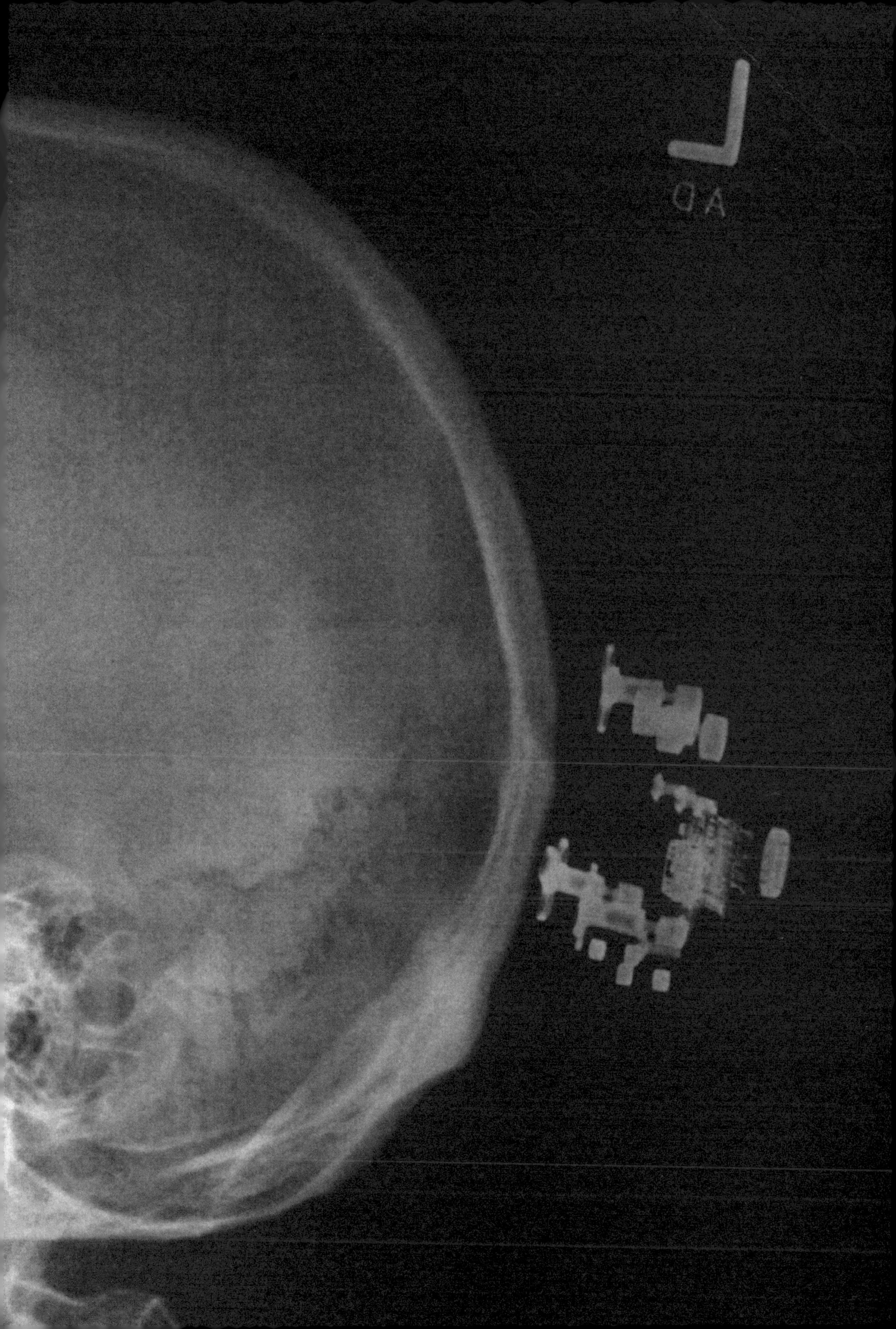
L

Gramercy MRI & Diagnostic Radiology, PC
380 2nd Avenue
New York, NY 10010
212-477-8180

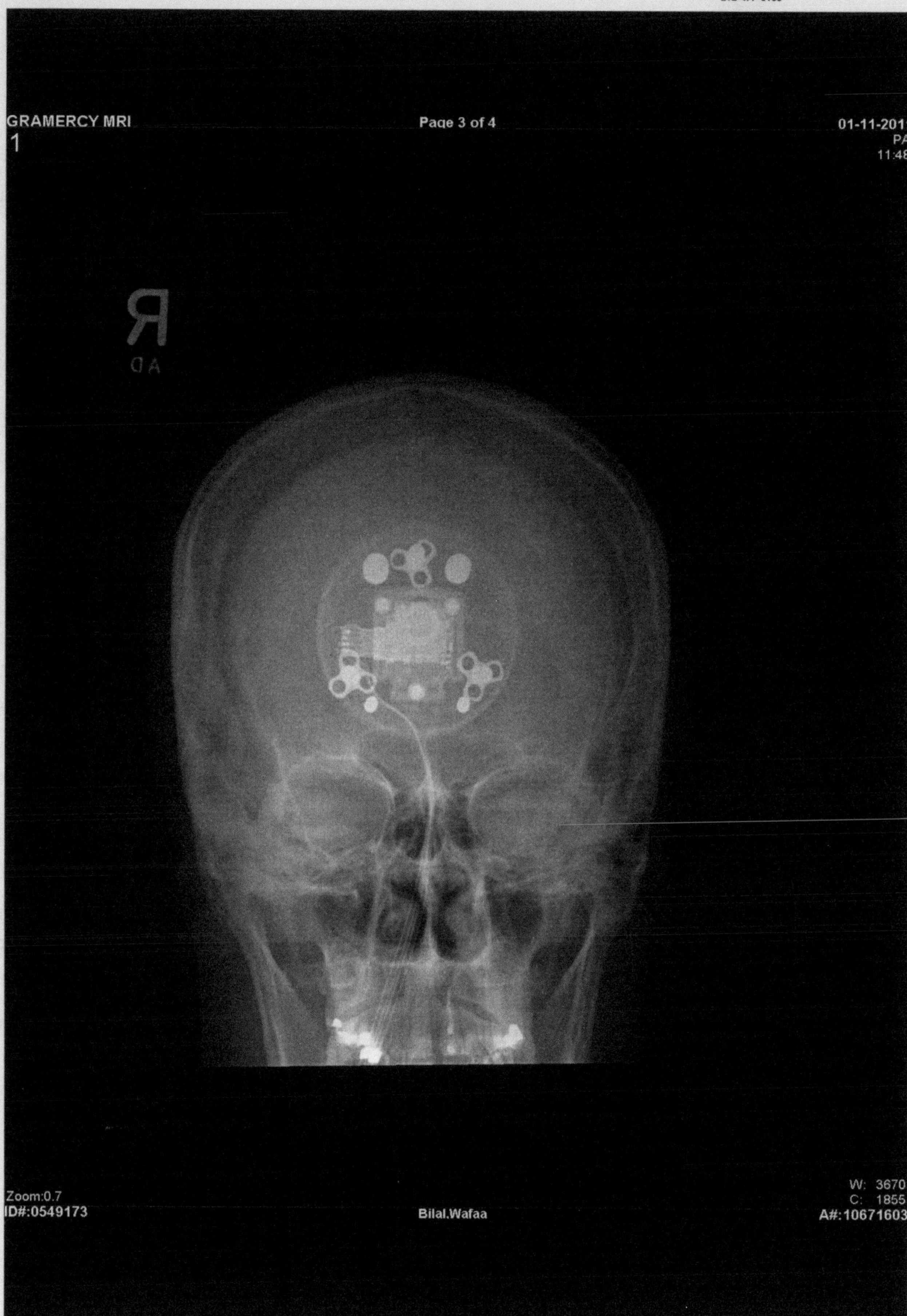

64–65 Wafaa Bilal in the early days of his *3rdi* performance, with the implanted camera in the back of his head visible as he walks through New York City's SoHo neighborhood.

66 Initial technical sketches of the *3rdi* camera apparatus and its installation plan. The artist produced these four illustrations, part of more than a dozen drawings made in preparation for the project, with his longtime collaborator Kevin McElroy.

67 Fellow Chicago-based artist Nyeema Morgan pours silicone rubber over Wafaa Bilal's head to create a mold, part of the extensive process of producing the *3rdi* camera implant. This process took place at Kodiak Studios in Brooklyn, New York.

68–69 An image taken by the *3rdi* camera on the final, 369th day of the *3rdi* performance. The image, like each photo taken by the camera implanted in the back of Bilal's head, was uploaded to a website that continues to function as a postperformance archive. Each image includes location data, the date, and the time; we can see here that Bilal was in Indonesia on December 18, 2011, at 6:39 am.

70–71 A selection of images taken by the *3rdi* camera. The performance produced an image every minute for its duration, generating more than half a million photographs.

72–74 X-rays taken on January 11, 2011, at Gramercy MRI and Diagnostic Radiology center in New York City. While undergoing the year-long performance, the artist had to maintain regular doctor visits due to various complications from the implant.

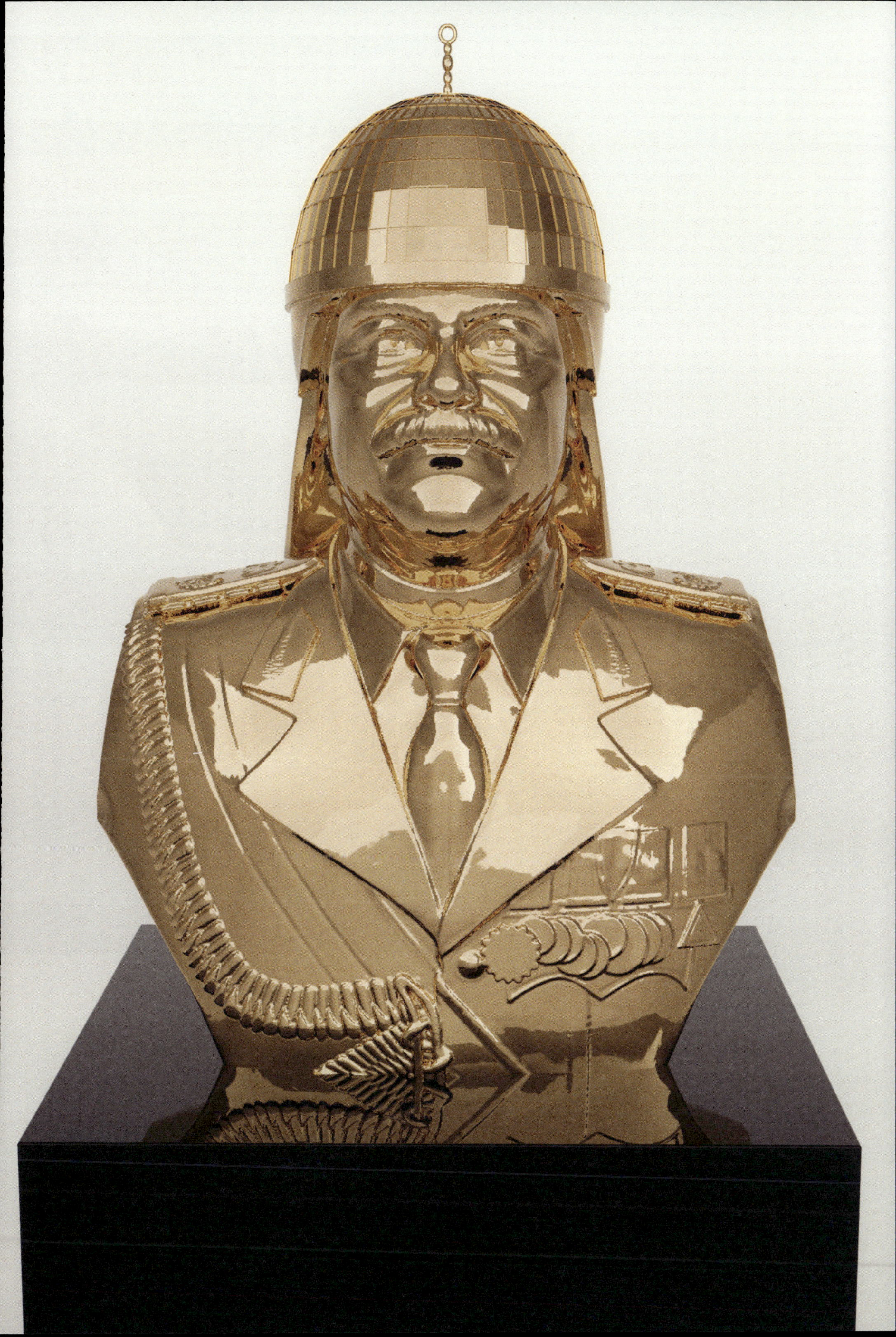

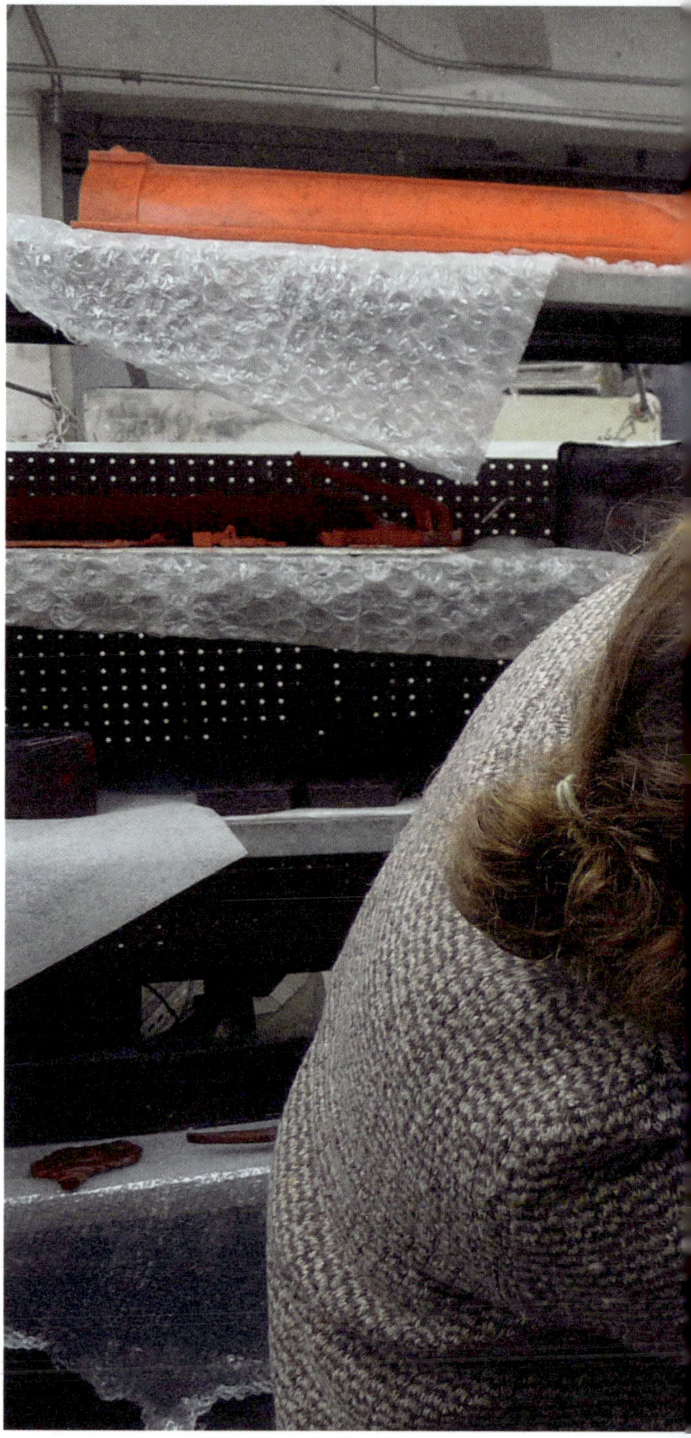

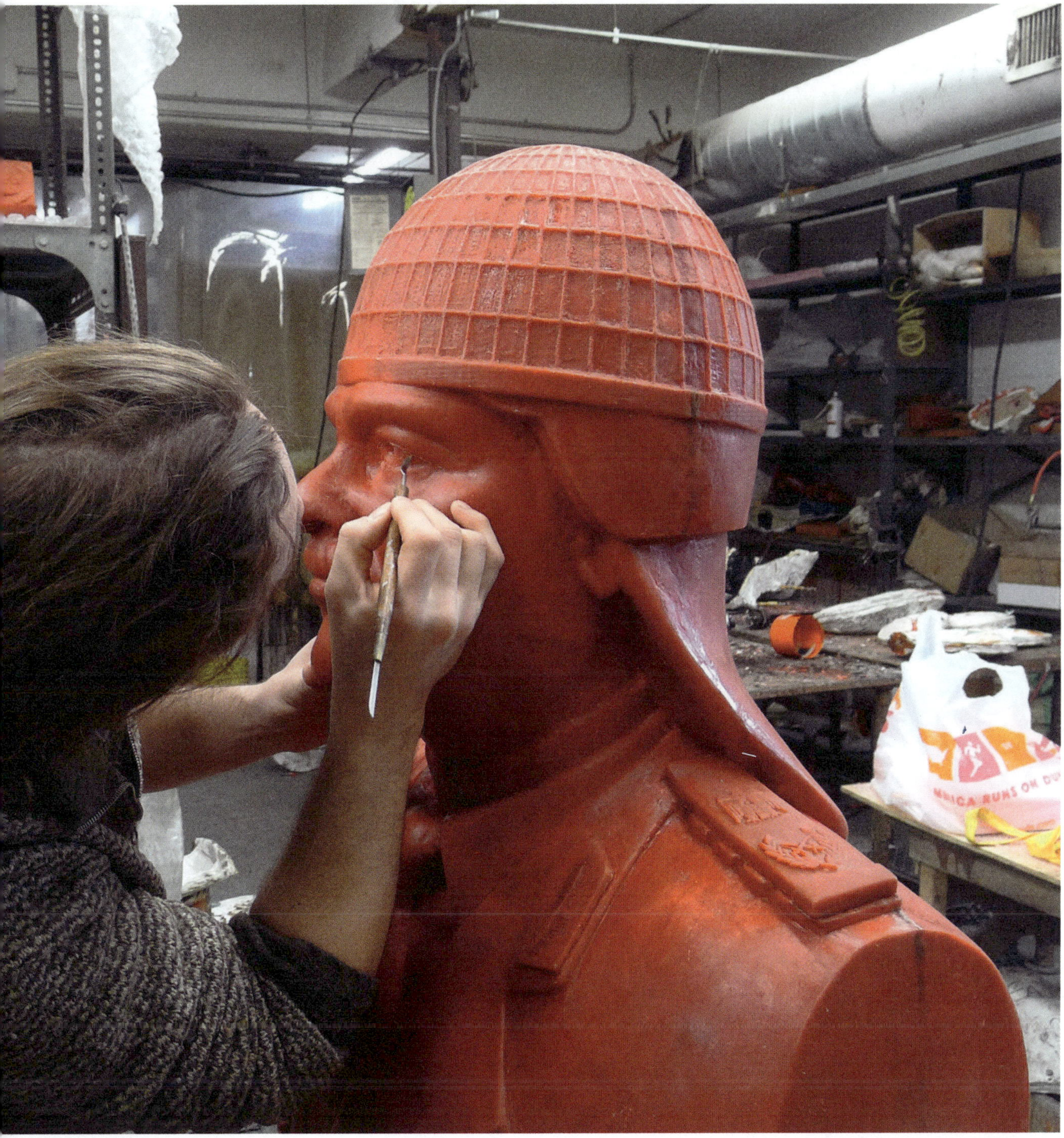

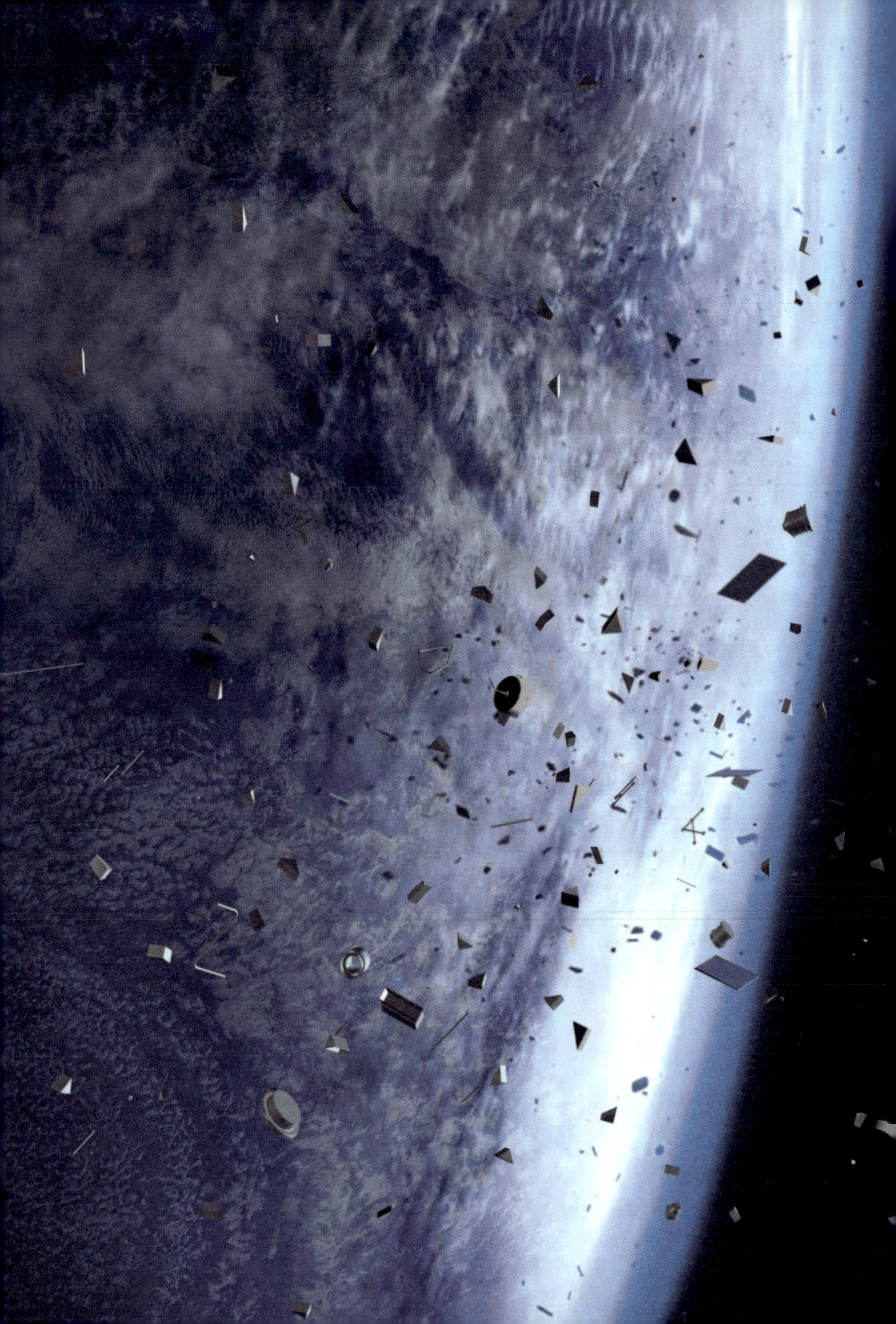

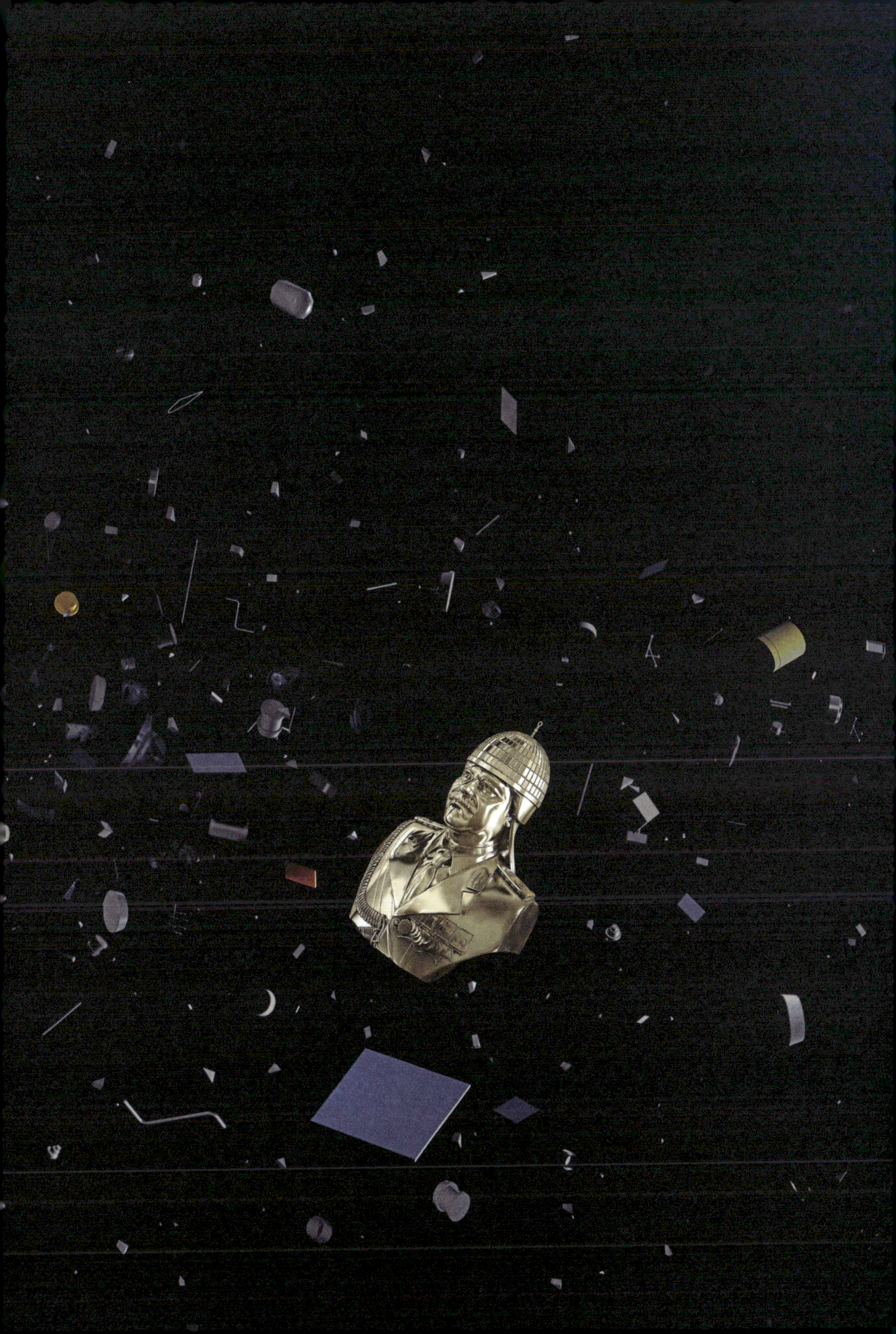

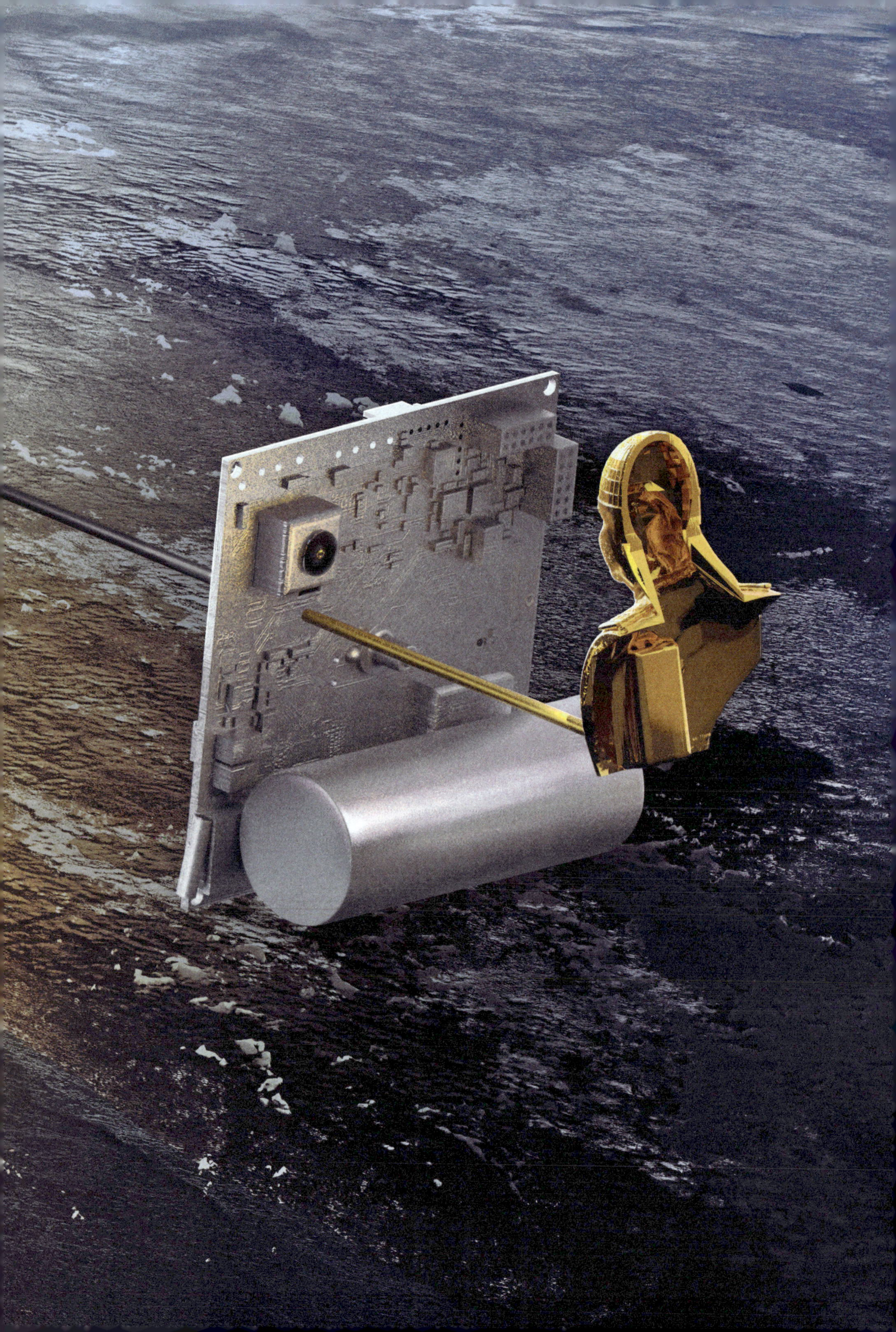

CANTO III, 2015
BRONZE WITH GOLD FINISH

77 Titled *Canto III*, this bronze bust with a gold finish depicts Saddam Hussein. It is a scaled-down replica of the 30-foot-high sculptures that once sat atop the palace of the former Iraqi president. This "antimonument" is one of the first in a series of works where Bilal reflects on Hussein's dictatorship and egotism.

78–79 The development of *Canto III* included a molding process (pictured here) followed by a casting. To fund the production of this work, Bilal launched a twenty-six-day Kickstarter campaign. Sixty people contributed to the campaign, enabling him to exhibit the work for the first time at the 2015 Armory show in New York.

SPACE JUNK, 2015
DIGITAL RENDERING

80–81 In the 1990s, Saddam Hussein's followers proposed a plan to launch a gold bust of their ruler into space as a tribute to his lasting power. This rendering from 2015 titled *Space Junk* is the first of many renderings that Bilal would make of Hussein's bust in space.

RENDERING OF THUMBSAT MODEL, 2024
DIGITAL RENDERING

82 More than three decades after the original planned tribute, Bilal is following through on sending a bust of Saddam Hussein into lower orbit. This detail of a rendering by Bilal was made in collaboration with ThumbSat, a company that will ultimately help realize the project in space.

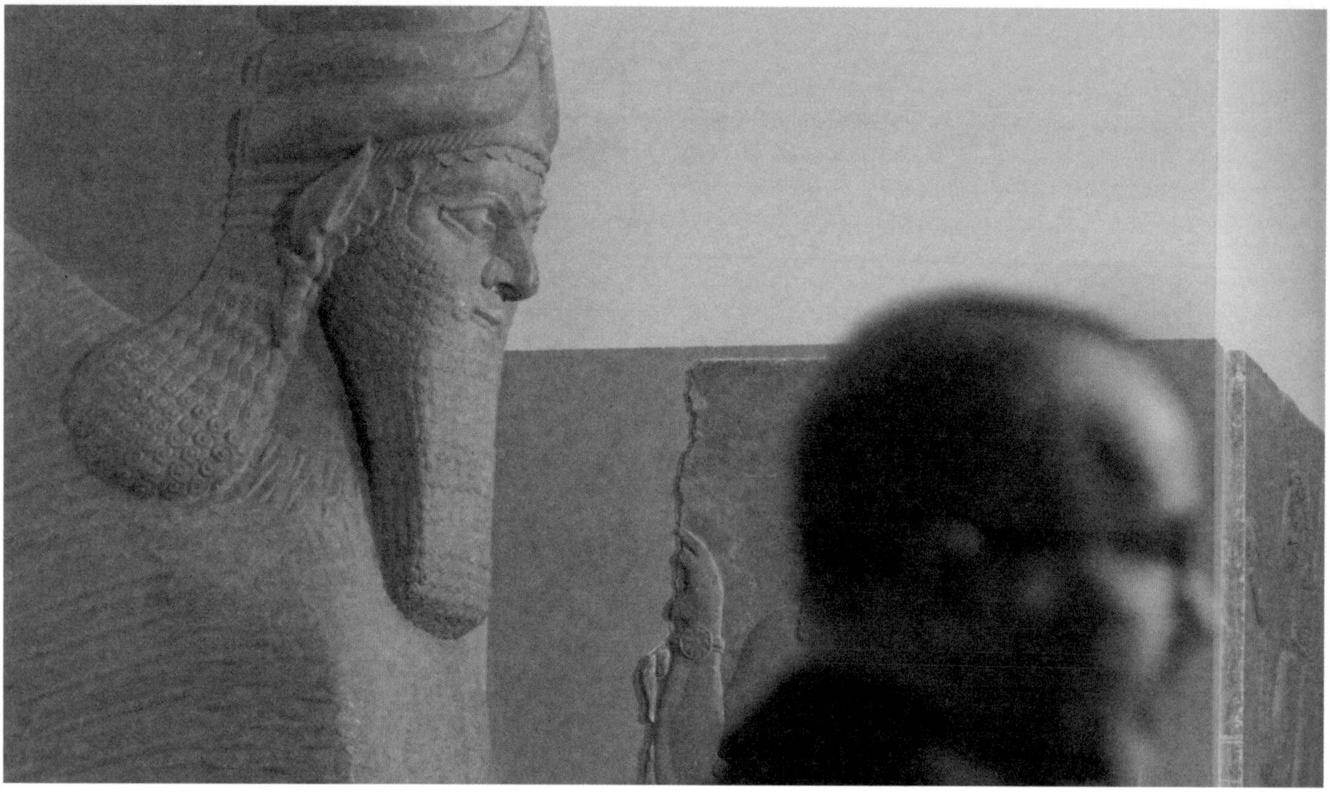

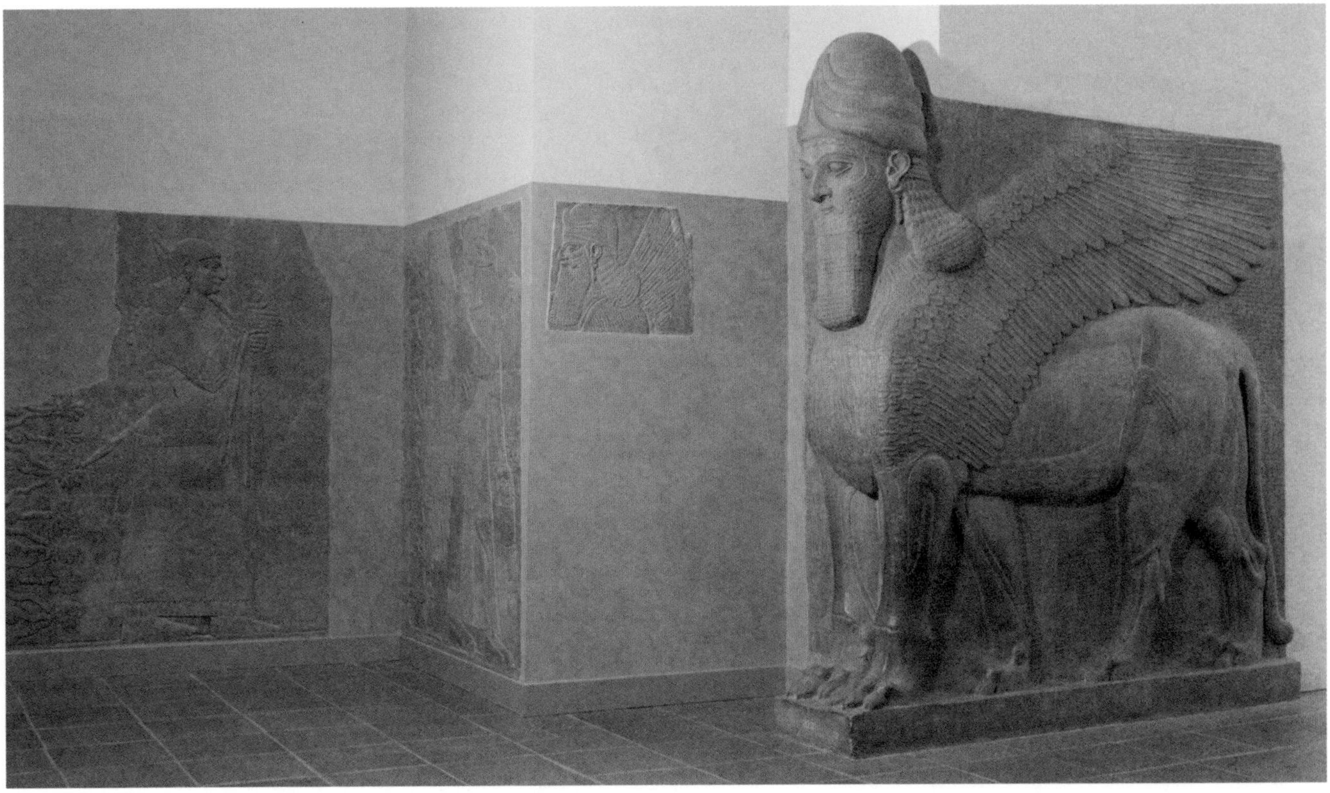

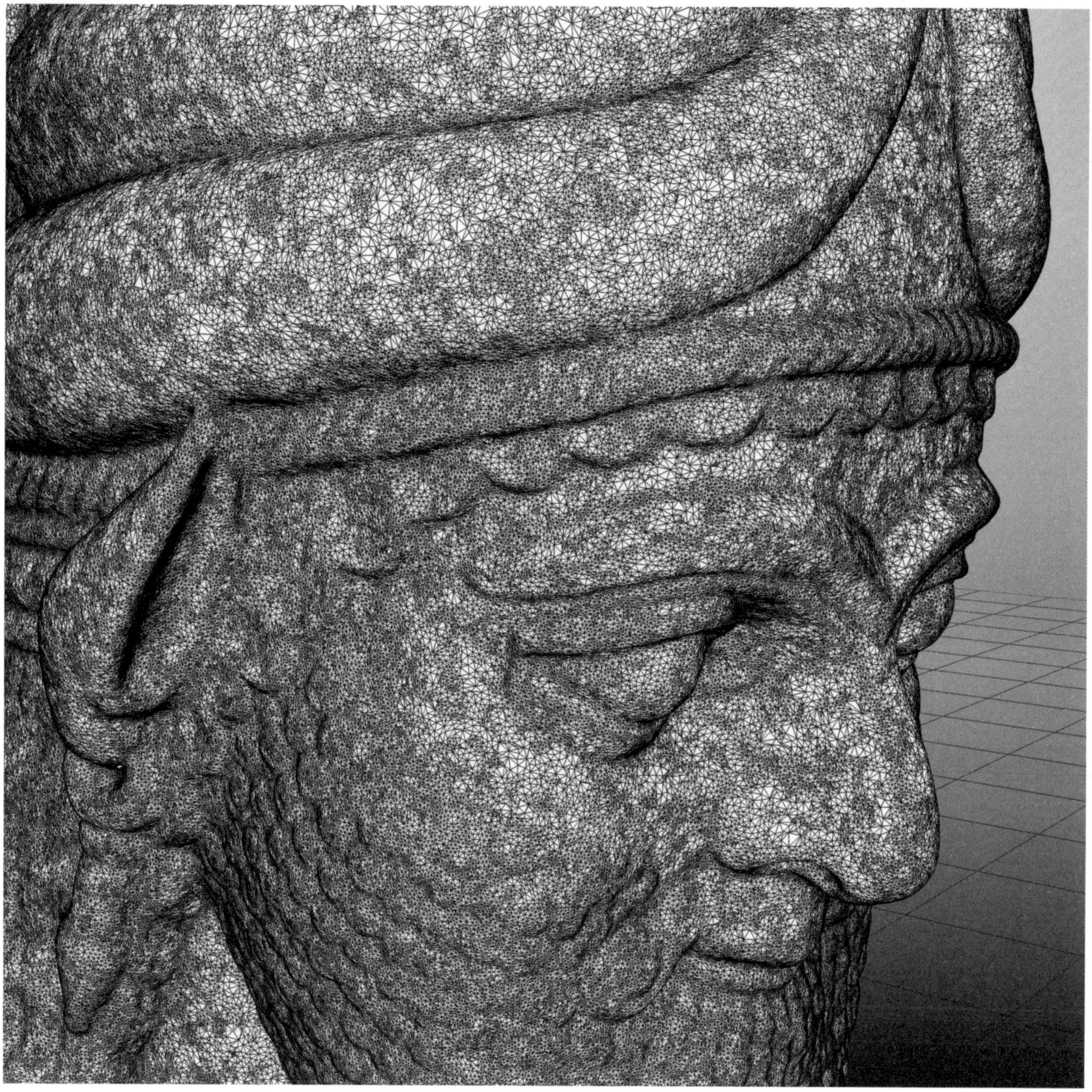

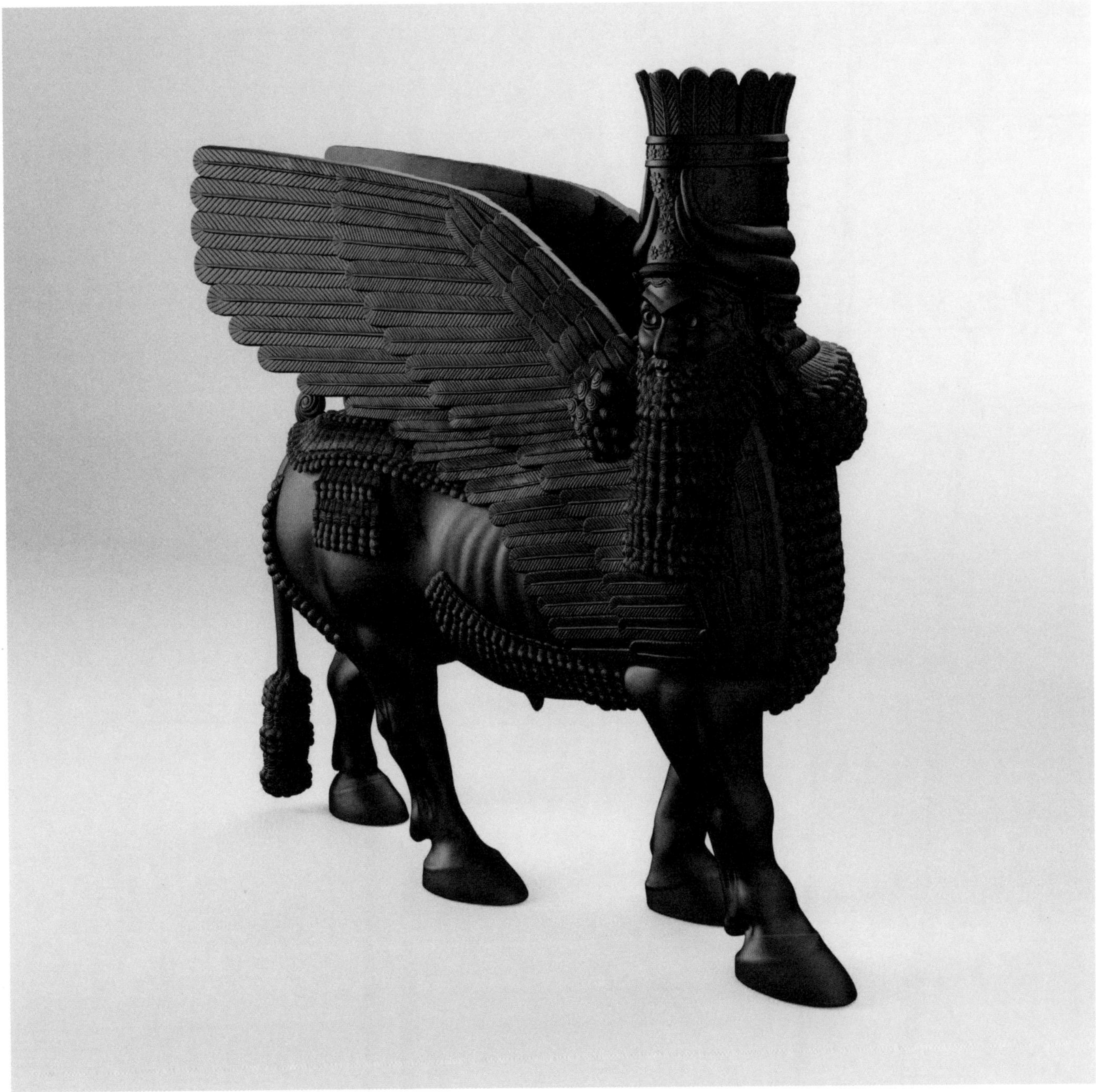

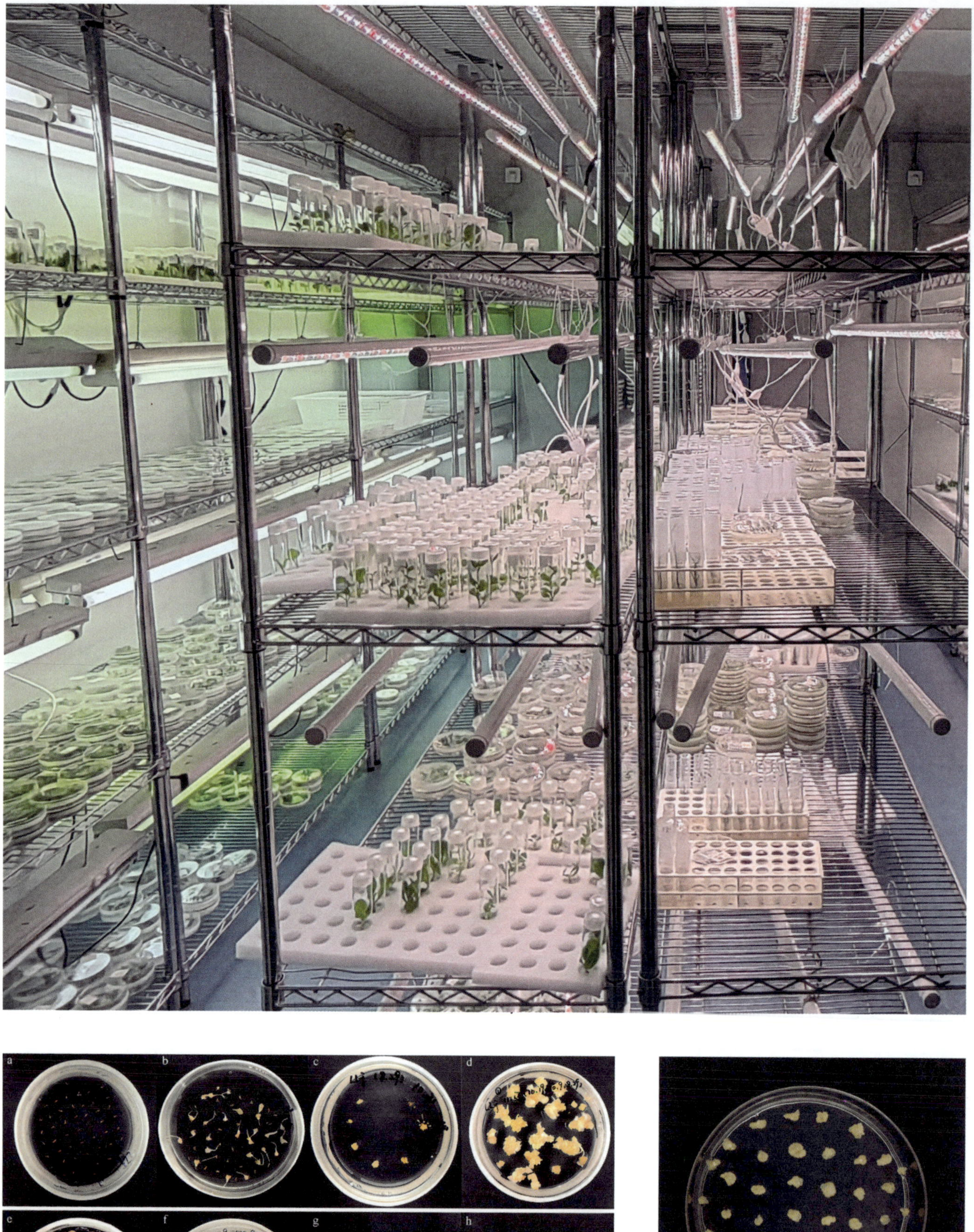

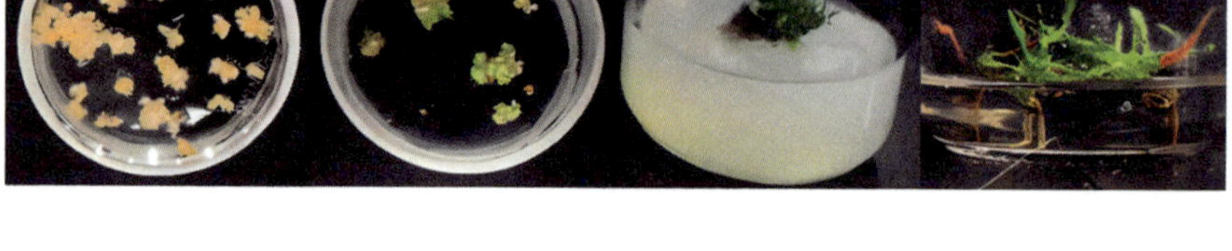
a
b
c
d
e
f
g
h

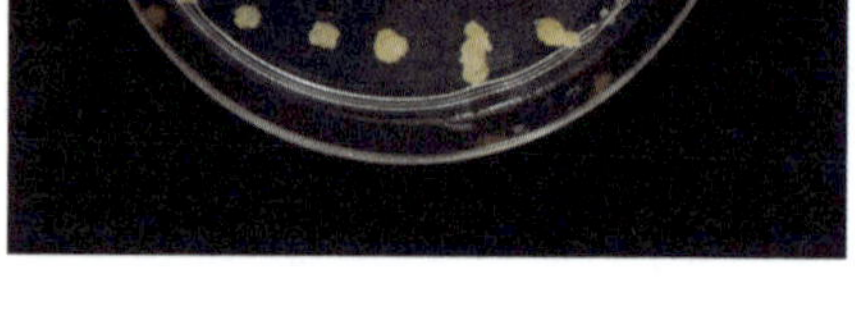

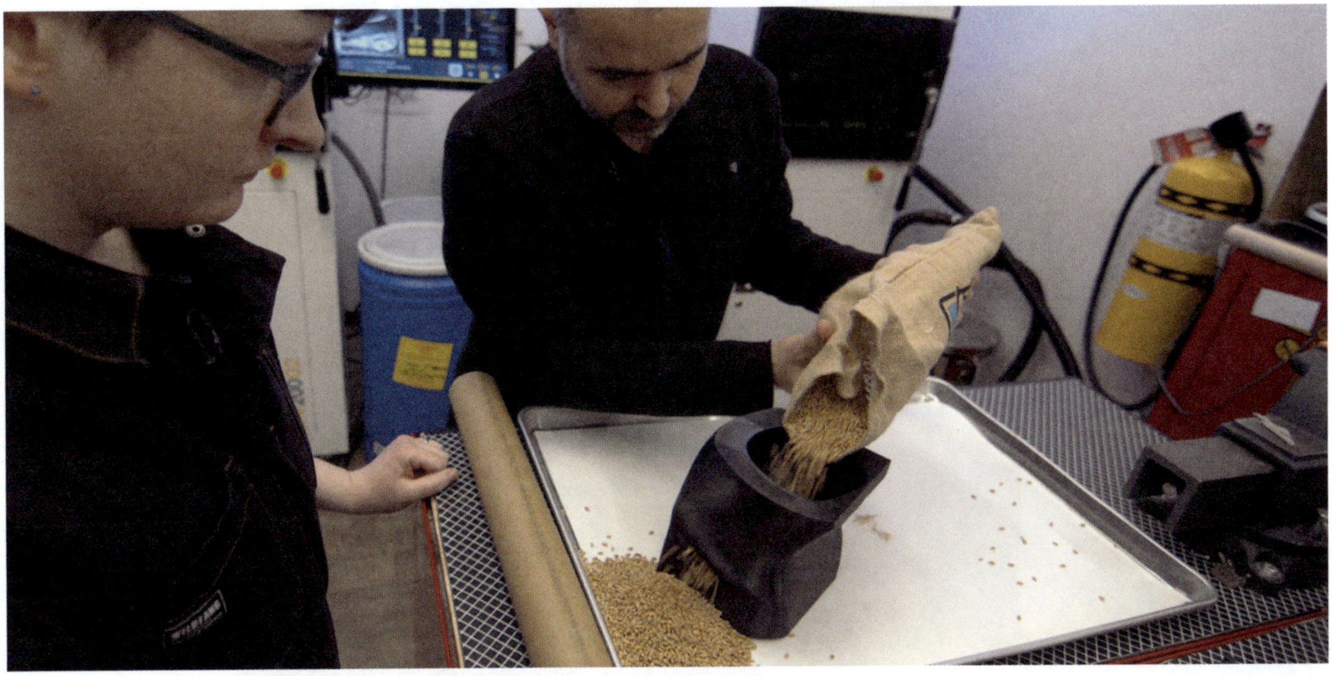

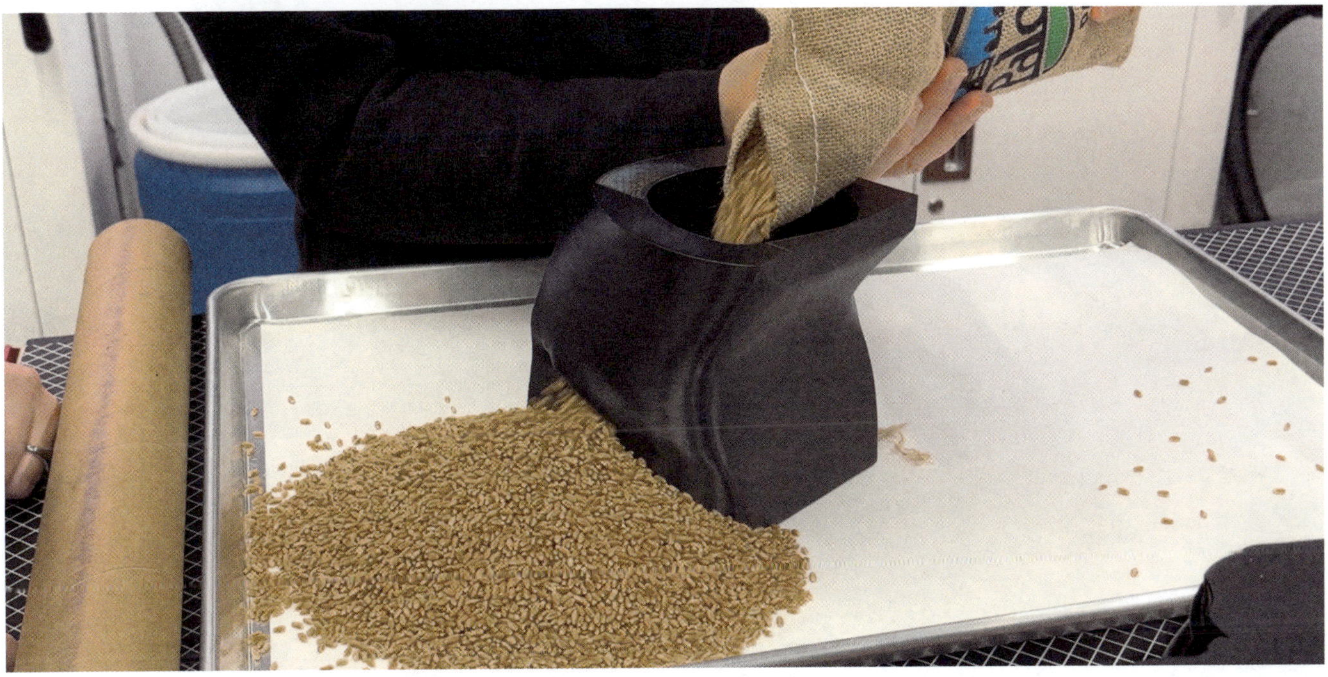

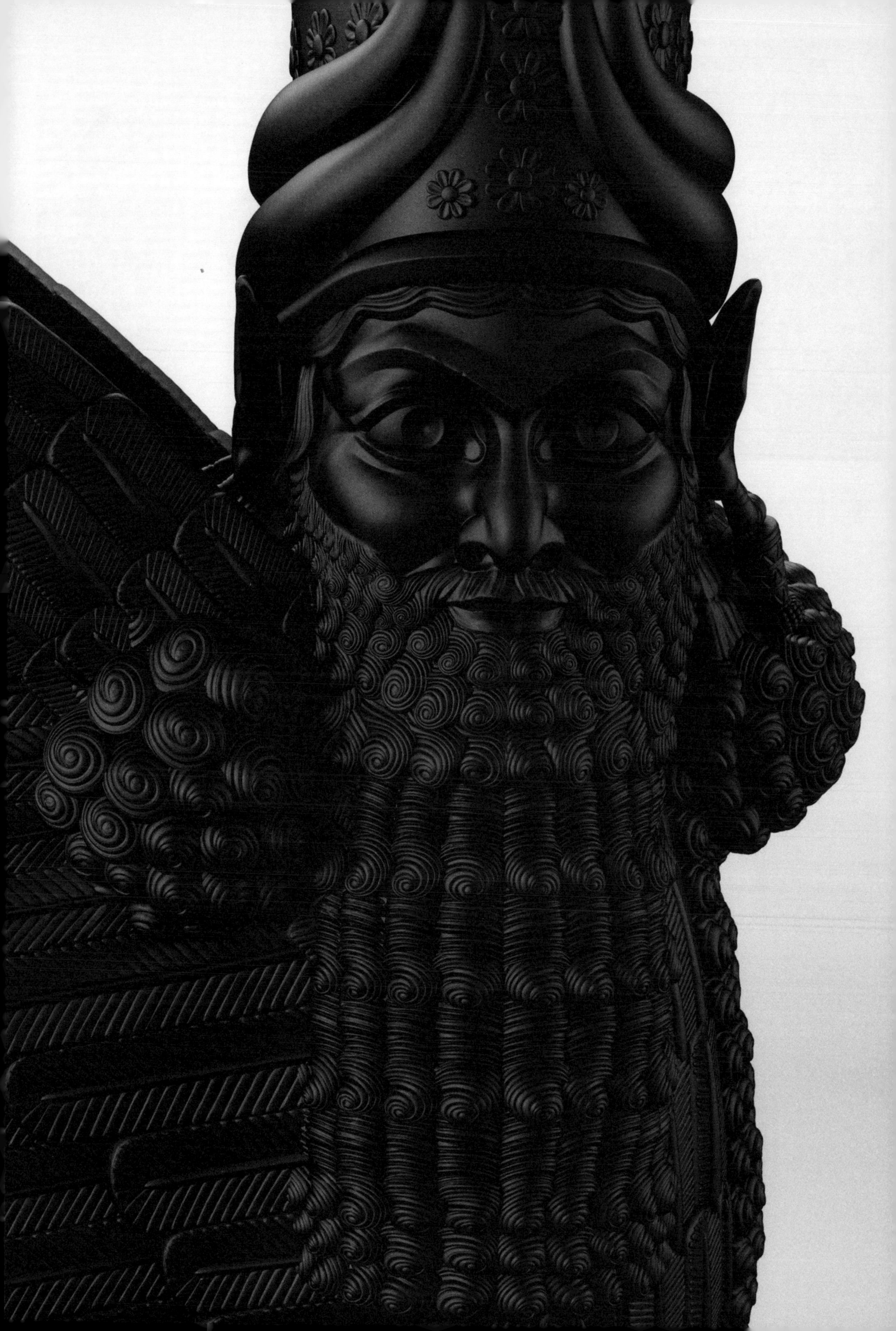

84–85 These images were captured during Bilal's visit to The Metropolitan Museum of Art on January 12, 2024. Originally from the ancient city of Nimrud, the pair of lamassus shown here are the sister sculptures to the lamassus that were targeted and destroyed by ISIS in modern day Mosul in 2015, a catalyzing event that prompted Bilal to create *In a Grain of Wheat*. The first step of the *In a Grain of Wheat* project entailed Bilal and a team of collaborators developing a detailed 3D scan of one of these two sculptures.

86 This computer rendering was made by Bilal's longtime collaborator Shawn Lawson in 2024. To produce it, Lawson used the Redshift program to custom-render the original 3D scan of the lamassu at the Met. This high resolution render simulates the Maya program's viewport rendering. The Lamassu 3D model is the basis for what was encoded into the bioengineered DNA of a wheat seed for the *In a Grain of Wheat* project.

87 Not to be confused with the 3D rendering Bilal created for *In a Grain of Wheat*, which depicted a front-facing lamassu in a stationary position, this digital rendering was made for the production of the 7-foot-tall, 3D-printed sculpture commissioned by the MCA, titled *Lamassu (In a Grain of Wheat)*. The lamassu Bilal selected for this sculpture is side-facing and portrays the lamassu in motion, as if walking forward. Bilal designed the front leg of the lamassu sculpture so that it could house the modified *In a Grain of Wheat* seeds, which would in turn spill from a slit at the base of the hoof (as shown on page 89).

88 These images from the tissue culture room at the biotechnology company Lifeasible show various moments from the plant transformation process that was undergone to cultivate the modified seeds for *In a Grain of Wheat*.

89 Here we see Bilal (right) with collaborator Dhemerae Ford (left) at New York University's LaGuardia Studio analyzing a prototype of the hoof for the MCA-commissioned *Lamassu (In a Grain of Wheat)* sculpture. Stored in an internal cavity within the lamassu's leg, the *In a Grain of Wheat* seeds are meant to spill out from a small slit in the front hoof of the sculpture.

90 Detail image of the stoic gaze from the rendering of the *Lamassu (In a Grain of Wheat)* sculpture, shown on page 87.

92–93 This sketch, which was drawn by Bilal's longtime collaborator James Kloiber, highlights a key interactive aspect of the MCA-commissioned *Lamassu (In a Grain of Wheat)* sculpture. The drawing shows a museum visitor bowing down to the sculpture and taking a few grains of wheat, which spill out, in a seemingly endless stream, from the front hoof.

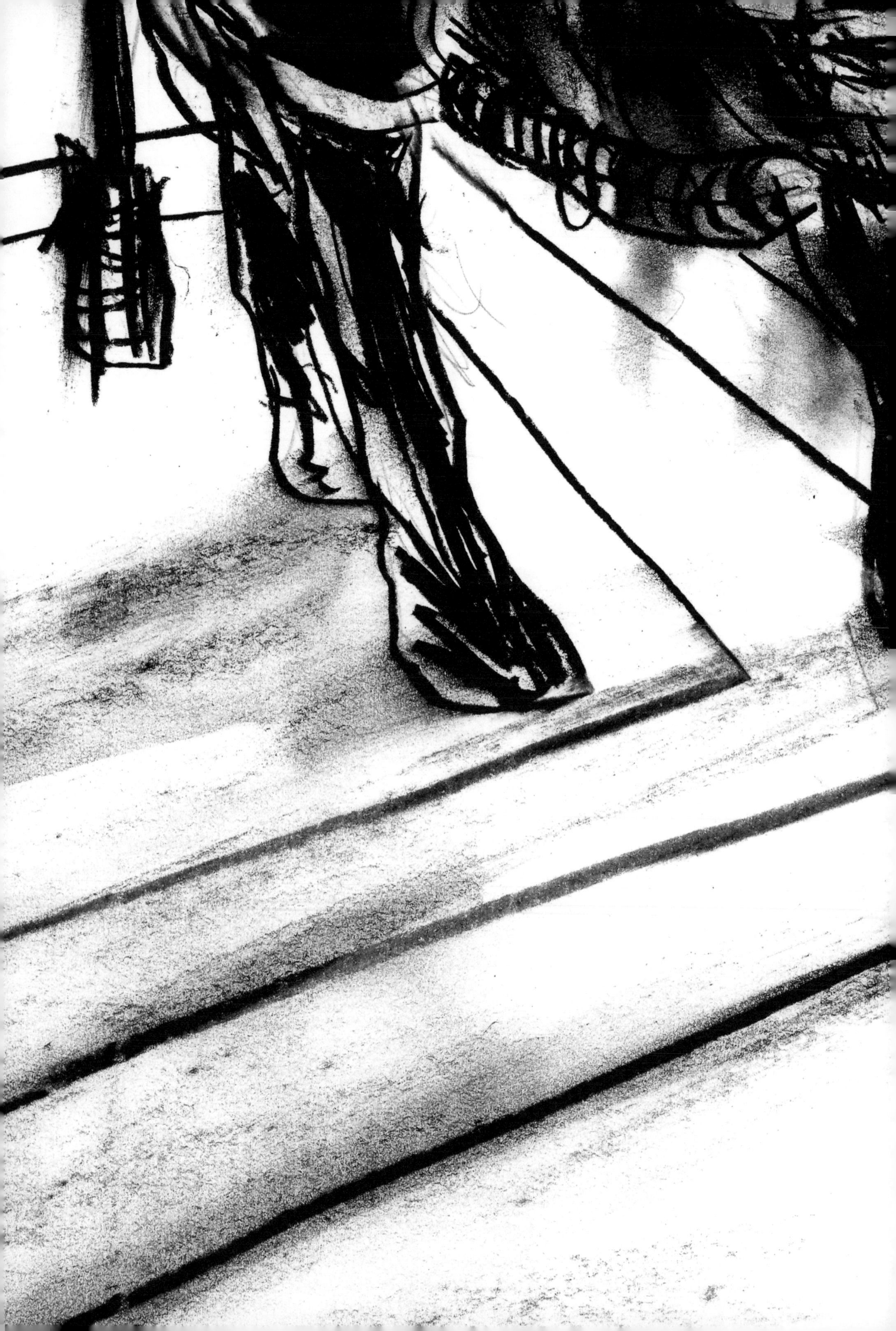

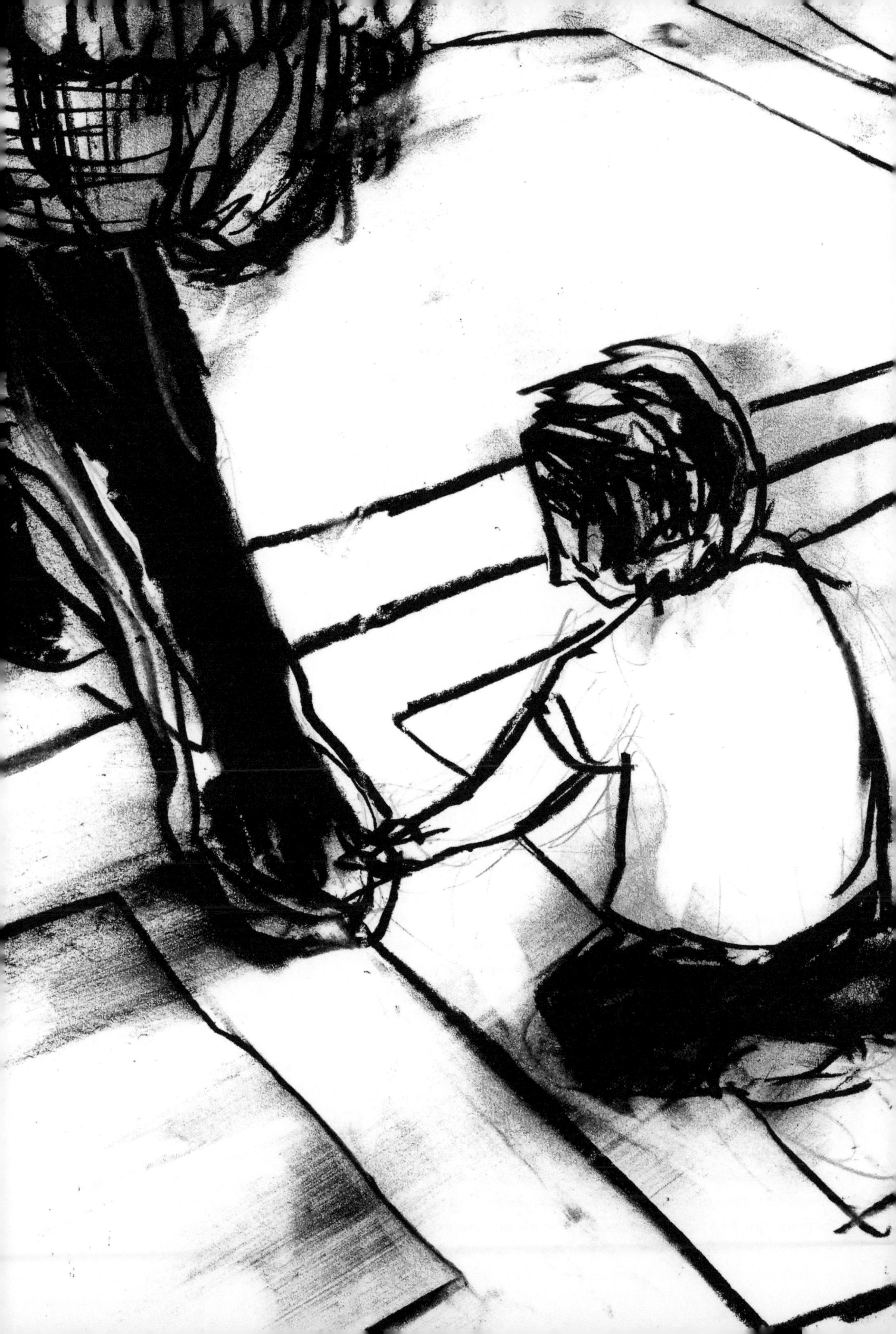

A Note from the Curator

Much of Wafaa Bilal's exhibition history is populated by single artwork displays—individual projects exhibited independently from other works. Such isolated installations are, in some sense, warranted, considering the complex and often participatory nature of his projects, not to mention the scale, both spatial and temporal, at which he operates. Just one work by Bilal can engage multiple disciplines, involve various modes of in-person and virtual interaction, and span years. This publication and its corresponding exhibition at MCA Chicago are an earnest attempt to shine a light on the throughlines and connections that emerge when you bring several of Bilal's visionary projects together—in this case, five works made over roughly the past two decades. To take such a long view of his practice is to see the ways he has artfully navigated the seemingly incomprehensible relationship between international and interpersonal politics. Also visible are the ways Bilal has resisted the erasure of a culture both by bringing attention to its destruction and, in turn, finding ways to resurrect that which has been lost. These and other connections have become integral to my understanding of Bilal's life and art, and my hope is that readers and visitors who are either new to Bilal's works or are only seeing them together for the first time will discover insights beyond those I have attempted to highlight here.

I would also like to take a moment to expand on the subtitle of this publication and exhibition, as it attests to another essential thread running through Bilal's work. *Indulge Me*, while on the surface a somewhat playful turn of phrase, is deployed here as both a reference to the metaphor of cannibalism that I've argued informs the artist's practice and an acknowledgment of the cannibalistic conditions of today's hyperconsumerist world. The exhibition begins with a metaphorical cannibalization of the human body as we observe Bilal leveraging his own body to interrogate power dynamics, particularly those that impact people marginalized by war or exploitation. Next, visitors encounter works that reflect on cultural profiteering and the consumption of Iraqi history and culture. Here, I hope visitors connect with contemporary conversations on reparations and the use of the arts in politics, whether for leverage, as a form of soft power, or for artwashing. The final work highlights Saddam Hussein's cannibalistic exploitation of Iraqi history, which relates to contemporary conversations on political ambition, propaganda, the performance of power, monuments, and megalomania.

Beyond the more obvious acts of consumption that inform our day-to-day existences, our contemporary vocabulary has become equally ripe with resemblance. We're starved for attention; we devour books and binge television; we're seemingly always hungry for more. To become aware of such language is, in a way, to think more consciously about the taking in of culture, whether our own or someone else's. So, as we flip through the pages of this book, or as we visit Bilal's works in the galleries at the MCA, perhaps we can ask ourselves: are we recognizing an artist whose work requires time, attention, and engagement, or are we coming to terms with our own indulgences? Perhaps, in the best circumstances, what we are doing is both.

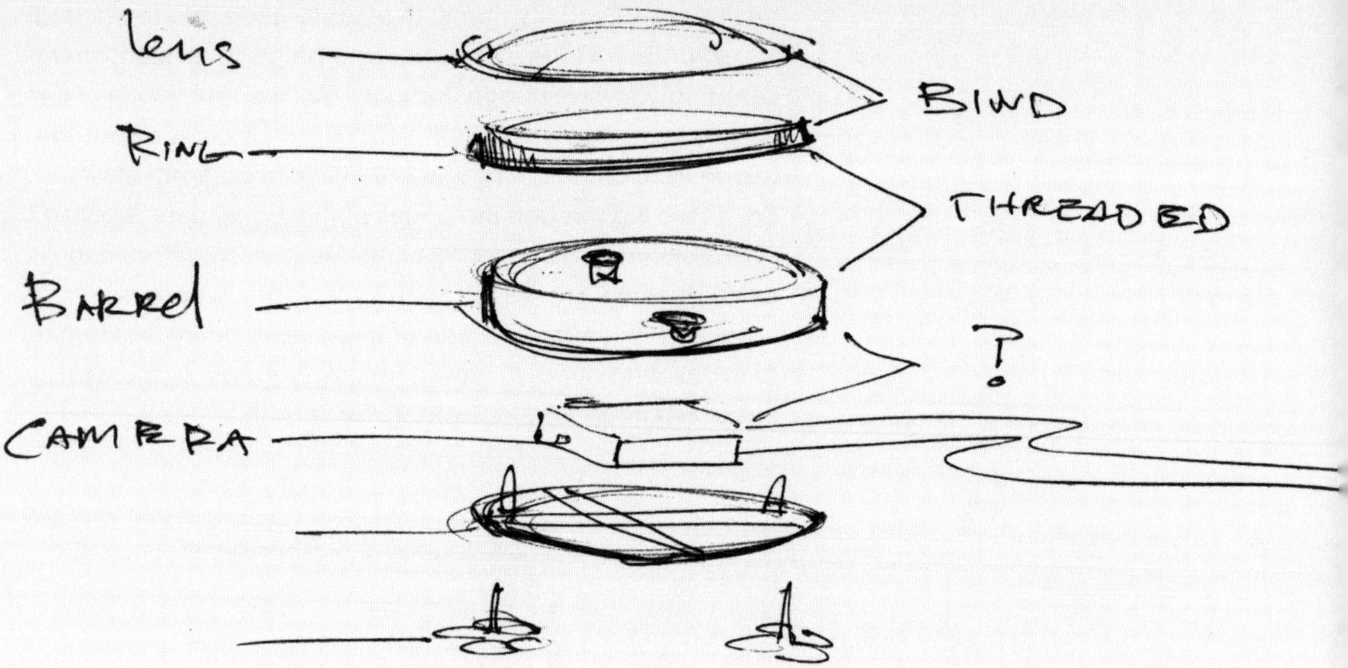
lens
RING
BIND
THREADED
BARREL
?
CAMERA

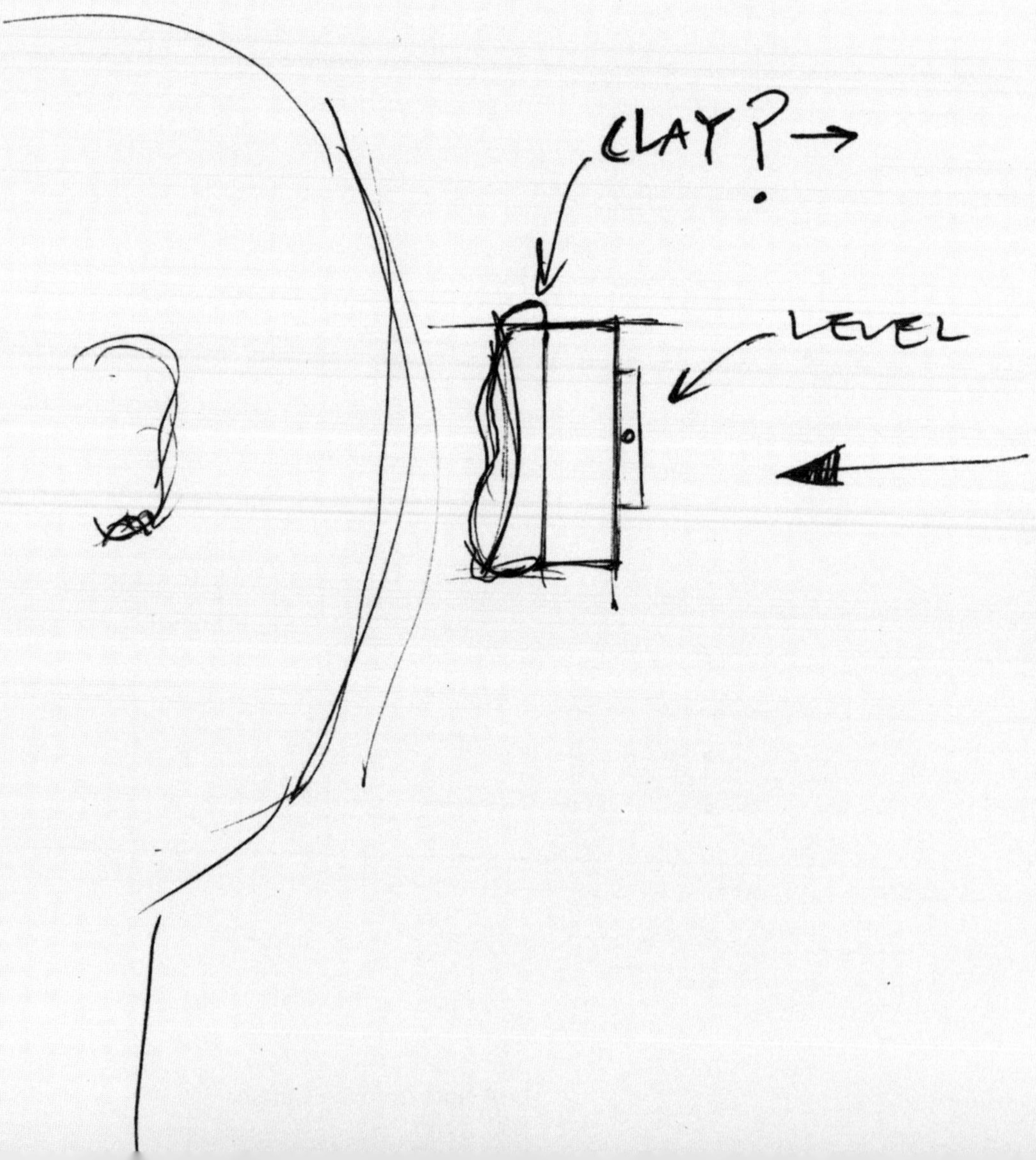
CLAY?
LEVEL

Art, Life, and Living

Wafaa Bilal

I arrived in the United States in shock, having experienced my own apocalypse.

I felt I had lost everything.

When I kissed my mother goodbye and left my home in Kufa, Iraq, in 1991, I could not even take a backpack. To do so might alert Saddam's authorities that I was on a journey, that I was trying to escape.

My journey started with seven days of walking toward the Kuwaiti border and forty-two days of hiding among the remnants of the Highway of Death, where American and allied forces ruthlessly bombed retreating Iraqi military and civilian vehicles following the failed 1990 invasion of Kuwait. I experienced a seeming eternity of rootlessness, anxiety, and fear, cowering in an abandoned vehicle, seeking shelter at an American military base, and eventually transferring to a refugee camp in Saudi Arabia.

The camp presented a brand-new hell: endless days stuck in limbo, as the camp descended into violence and chaos. Making art in the camp with whatever supplies I could find was the only thing that helped me survive. Without it, I wouldn't have been able to transform the horrors I'd experienced into something beautiful, into something meaningful. Art gave me hope, and, along with the generosity of sympathetic aid workers, helped me get out of the camp after two long years. That's when I landed in another desert: New Mexico.

I arrived in Albuquerque shell-shocked and reeling, trying to comprehend and communicate all the atrocities I had experienced. Atrocities that were still going on in the refugee camp and in my home country. Atrocities my family still faced every day. Atrocities that were stoked by the United States' intervention in Iraq.

There, in the relative comfort zone of New Mexico, I encountered a population that was largely unaware and oblivious to the things I had just survived. In some ways, I was in the belly of the beast, but the people surrounding me had no idea. It was bewildering, to say the least.

SCREAMING INTO A DEAFENING SILENCE

The floodgates of my emotions were flung open, and yet I felt like I was screaming into a deafening silence. I soon realized

I couldn't just scream. I had to *do something* to make people aware of what I had witnessed, experienced, and internalized. And to reflect it through myself, and through my art.

During my studies at the University of New Mexico, I wanted to bring viewers into a subject they were seemingly uninterested in. Because they were lacking a connection to Iraq, my work came across as aggressive and shocking; an image of a desperate man—myself—in the desert, wailing into a void. A hollow wooden crucifix opened to reveal a phallus wrapped in an American flag.

During these early years as a politically motivated artist, I was naive to the corrosive effects of antagonism as both a tactic and mode of engagement. My initial instinct was to confront the viewer and trigger an emotional experience, thus I took beloved cultural symbols—the flag, the cross—and filtered them through my experience of conflict. I altered the objects' original meanings to elicit a visceral response.

Art, after all, is about assigning a code to an object or a performative act. In this case, I assigned novel codes to common cultural objects, encasing them with new meaning to achieve my objective: to plead for attention to the conflict in Iraq that defined my reality—one that seemed too distant and absent to those around me.

My approach was fueled by the alienation and racism I experienced in this new land, and unfortunately, the outcome created a negative feedback loop that pushed people toward further resentments. I wanted to engage and inform my audience but I ended up disengaging them. This early approach may have seemed cynical or calculated, but it came from a place of sincerity, struggle, and longing.

Antagonism as a pursuit of engagement is a perverse quest for human connection. However, engaging through antagonism was preferable to hearing the echo of my scream coming back to me.

A NEW LOCATION AND A NEW RESPONSE

When I left New Mexico and arrived in Chicago in 2001, I found the same kinds of racism, ignorance, and disengagement from those around me.

But my own response had evolved.

By this point, I had recognized the failure of antagonism, and how it leads to alienation rather than connection. I was also beginning to understand the feelings of confinement and limitation that accompanied the relatively small, privileged world of galleries and museums. As an artist attempting to maneuver those spaces, I felt all too well my strain against them. I knew I needed a fresh strategy, so I turned to interactivity to build a platform for engagement. Technology would be my medium, my way to break the isolation of the white cube—the gallery—and enter everyday spaces.

Around this time, however, history would submit its own catalyzing event. A month after I moved to Chicago, the planes hit the World Trade Center.

I watched the terror unfold on a small TV in my studio apartment in Lakeview, and I knew the world would never be the same. Just walking the few blocks around the School of the Art Institute of Chicago, people would call me "Bin Laden." In their eyes, I was intrinsically linked to an attack that had nothing to do with my country or my history, except for the United States' own role. As patriotism and xenophobia were roiling my new home, I sought to create work that would convey the results of the last fifty years of American aggression in the world.

That work became a project for the School of the Art Institute's Jackson Gallery in Chicago: *Al Qaeda R Us*. In an otherwise empty room, the famous image from World War II of figures raising a flag in Iwo Jima was projected onto one of two interactive video screens. When a visitor walked into the room, the static image came to life, the American flag rippling. I recall one young woman strolling in and planting herself below the flag—an innocent witness to America's aggression abroad, seeing what so many Americans continued to ignore. The other screen showed archival and contemporary footage of US intervention from around the world, accompanied by an eerie piano composition from one of my colleagues—a repetitive single note evoking the tolling of a bell or a ticking bomb. *Ajrass* rang in my head (pp. 116–17).

Looking back, *Al Qaeda R Us* was didactic in approach, but it was also interactive and poetic. With it, I was beginning to understand *interactivity* instead of *reactivity*, as well as the possibilities opened up by technology. I was also starting to feel that I could live without war constantly defining me, that I could leave the conflict zone inhabiting my mind and ease into the relative comfort of life in the United States.

WHEN THE PERSONAL BECOMES POLITICAL

In 2004, that feeling was shattered by another personal tragedy.

My brother Haaji was killed in Iraq by a drone. He was stationed at a makeshift checkpoint at Kufa Bridge near our home, as many young men did in those days as American forces advanced.

Every dimension of my existence—my art, life, vitality—collapsed violently into one painful mass. Every fiber of my being and every moment of my time were melded together as I struggled to make sense of this new loss, foisted upon me just as I had been starting to adapt to my new reality.

Like so many other young men in Iraq, Haaji was driven to militancy by the intervention of the United States in our country, and he was killed by a drone of the type piloted by US soldiers from thousands of miles away, from total safety and comfort.

Hajji was actually a term that US soldiers used flippantly to refer to Iraqi men, denying them individuality and humanity. To the United States, my brother was just another *Hajji*, not Haaji.

Haaji's death left me no choice, no doubt: My artwork had to be political. I could not separate events halfway around the world from my present reality in the United States. Struggling to make sense of these senseless losses, art became my only path forward.

Even as I was overwhelmed with fury and frustration, something was beginning to change in the United States. There was room to question the Iraq War. There was a growing anti-war movement, and people were ready to hear my point of view, ready to engage. And engage them I did. I created *Domestic Tension*, otherwise known as *Shoot an Iraqi*, a project centered around my brother's death and my own vulnerability and dissonant reality.

For a month, I sequestered myself in a small Chicago gallery with a paintball gun that people could aim and fire at me from anywhere in the world via the internet. I was living constantly under fire, trying to survive mentally and physically while ducking behind the furniture in my makeshift room, always anticipating the painful blasts and physical impacts from the paintball gun, which blanketed the room in dripping bursts of sickly yellow paint.

In total, the gun was fired at me over 65,000 times. People could chat and comment as they watched and fired. The project tore open a view into human nature and into cultures more violent, but also more heartening, than I had ever expected. By making myself vulnerable and asking people to directly participate in a quasi act of war, I was inviting them to confront the reality of conflict in such places as Iraq and their own proclivity for participation—as an aggressor or as a protector. Not only did people fire the gun at me, a movement also emerged to protect me, with individuals online turning the gun away even as others tried to train it on me. It was a virtual ballistic tug-of-war. The online comments were heart-wrenching and soul-baring, and some comments even translated to in-person contact. For example, a former US Marine visited me to bring a new lamp after mine was destroyed by the gun, a pragmatic act of compassion and kindness.

I emerged from the project exhausted, traumatized, and imbued with a new understanding of human beings, my new home in the comfort zone of the United States, and the possibilities for my own art. I also was alerted to the potential for using my own body to generate empathy.

A NEW LEXICON OF PERFORMANCE AND CONNECTION

Performance is a largely unmediated art form and yields power through its immediacy.

While my previous projects focused on the power of antagonism as a medium for communication, as my interests evolved so too did my belief in the power of performance to generate pathos. By centering the body, performance creates a relational and immediate encounter between the artist and the viewer, thus stimulating a profound human connection.

I applied this new vocabulary to my next major project, *The Iraqi House*. At the Montalvo Arts Center in Saratoga, California, I enlisted the community to help build a traditional Iraqi home by hand. Working together, we molded bricks out of local sand and mud, constructing the structure piece by piece, investing our sweat in fellowship.

Unbeknownst to my fellow workers, the plan was to destroy the house, suddenly and violently, as so many homes in Iraq were demolished. The center's administration, however, would not permit the destruction of the house, undermining the intention of my work. At that point in my career, I had no interest in creating permanent objects, and the inability to destroy the house eliminated the process of creating a platform for open engagement. In frustration, I walked away from the project and the now-meaningless object.

Meanwhile, the death toll in Iraq continued to mount—even years after President George W. Bush had declared "mission accomplished" aboard the USS *Abraham Lincoln* in 2003—and the need to put my body on the line only intensified. This need not only emerged out of a drive to engage with others, but also in an effort to process my own trauma, exorcise my demons, and confront my survivor's guilt. As my life in Iraq receded further into the distance, I grappled with the concept of an ever-present yet ever-disappearing past.

Thus, *3rdi* was born.

In 2008, I made the leap to New York with a teaching position at New York University. Over time, New York City has become more than just a workplace. It is my second home, and it has been the backdrop for countless art projects, including *3rdi*.

For the work, a small camera was surgically embedded in my head, forever gazing behind me, capturing a constant stream of images. Those images were uploaded automatically and live-streamed to the website 3rdi.me, capturing a live and permanent record of everything I walked away from or left behind: the mundane, the meaningful, the playful, the painful. It might be the blank wall behind me as I read; a busy street in New York as I strolled to my studio; or a mosaic of palm trees and blazing sunlight when I visited Mathaf: Arab Museum of Modern Art in Doha, Qatar, to unveil the project.

For one year I lived with *3rdi*, always conscious of its presence, from the dull pain in my skull that never receded to the stream of images that were both familiar and foreign as they unfolded behind me. Today, of course, streaming images and video are commonplace, but at the time it was novel technology—so novel that I was required to carry a small laptop with me at all times to directly upload the images online.

Certainly, this act was imbued with cultural significance, extending well beyond a technological exploration. Many Muslims and Middle Easterners are surveilled constantly by the US government, a cruel collective punishment since the attacks on 9/11. With *3rdi* I returned that gaze, uploading my private life onto a public platform—every minute for an entire year—inviting the public to watch my life even as my *3rdi* watched those around me. A poetic yet painful gaze.

My antagonism phase had long since receded, and I had embraced both the body and the poetic gesture to drive empathy, engagement, and reflection. I was ready for yet more action. I wanted to play a direct role in cultivating a postconflict world, rebuilding our traumatized societies and psyches.

A VETERAN OF STRUGGLE

In Iraq as in the United States, young people with wealth and privilege were not the ones dying. I had seen so many of my friends and relatives sent to the front lines in Iraq to die, against their wishes, through conscription or in desperate attempts to feed their families or fight for misguided ideologies. Demagogues would call them heroes, but they were not treated as heroes when, or if, they returned to civil society. The perpetrators and the survivors, the killers and the dead, were all victims of war, caught up in brutal battles orchestrated by powers far beyond their control.

As I contemplated such realities, I gained increasing empathy for US soldiers and veterans, who experienced some of the same trauma and exploitation that my own people had so long suffered. I yearned to work directly with US veterans, to understand their struggles and build bridges between our worlds.

Among my offerings was *Canto III*.

Like many dictators, Saddam Hussein was obsessed with immortality and deification. He had countless regal statues and likenesses of himself created and installed across the country so that we felt constantly watched by this unwelcome visage. His Ba'ath Party even had the dream of launching a gold bust of Saddam into orbit to forever watch over the world.

I sought to demystify and deflate Saddam's visions of grandeur, and to do so I enlisted the help of US veterans. Together we constructed a repository of mundane household goods and trinkets, each one a replica of the towering effigy of Saddam crowned with the holy shrine of the Dome of the Rock, intended by his supporters to signify his divine mandate. Our mass creations of this visage turned the bust into a mockery of itself, Saddam's power obliterated by familiarity and contempt. We negated the power of the dictator by reclaiming and commodifying his image into candlesticks and bookends.

For the final stage of this ongoing project, I will realize the Ba'ath Party's dream of sending a bust of Saddam into orbit. This satellite, however, will transform his vision of immortality into a kitschy, comedic object, a golden bust only one-inch tall. The *Canto III* satellite will be sent into a low orbit so that it will not circle the earth indefinitely, nor will it become space junk. Rather, it will tumble into the atmosphere and disintegrate.

A poetic ending for a megalomaniac.

A BLANK SLATE

Even though Saddam's regime and ideology had receded in the years following his demise, and even though many in Iraq, including my family, could live and work without daily fear of violence, the country was still in shambles—physically, psychologically, and emotionally. Iraqis had lived in isolation for so many years, fighting for their lives as the artifacts and archives of one of the globe's richest and oldest cultures were destroyed around them.

In the thirteenth century, the invading Mongols threw all the books from Baghdad's Bayt al-Hikmah library into the Tigris River to create a bridge to cross. In this tale I was told as a child, the water ran blue with ink for seven days, washing all the knowledge and history into the river. Similarly, so much of Iraq's patrimony was destroyed—literally *and* symbolically—during the 2003 invasion. Among other losses, the College of Fine Arts library at the University of Baghdad was looted and burned, countless priceless books obliterated. In all, 70,000 titles were lost. I wanted to raise awareness of this travesty, and also help the library literally rebuild.

Hence, *168:01*.

One hundred and sixty-eight hours represents the seven days the Tigris ran blue with ink eight centuries ago, and one second marks the start of our rebuilding. I worked with the College of Fine Arts to develop a list of books needed to restore their collection, and I enlisted supporters across the world to supply these tomes through an exchange wherein the supporters received one of the symbolically blank, all-white books I created in my own library.

I exhibited this white library internationally, a chilling participatory monument to all the knowledge lost, and simultaneously a clean slate offering hope for revival and resilience. Today, more than 13,000 books have been sent to Iraq through the *168:01* exchange.

THE DNA OF ANTIQUITY

The loss of books in the thirteenth century and during the recent war are only two examples of a tragic history of the devastation of knowledge and culture in Iraq. My country's epic history of war, invasion, imperialism, colonialism, and, more recently, terrorism, has given it a portfolio of cultural destruction almost as outstanding as its legacy of civilization.

When ISIS swept through Iraq in its fundamentalist reign of terror, it violently destroyed the ancient town of Nimrud. I was devastated by this act of violence. The stories of our ancestors make our lives and cultures richer. Stories and traditions, however, can vanish or be forgotten as one generation moves to the next. Cultural relics, sculptures, and antiquities are the tangible representation of how we once lived. Stories are embedded in these historical artifacts, and once these references disappear, there are intergenerational consequences of cultural erasure. This is the unfortunate aim of fundamentalists and extremists such as ISIS, or imperialists and colonizers across time. Priceless antiquities are often targeted and destroyed in an attempt to attack tradition and to replace it with a new ideology, new iconography.

I struggled to grapple with the loss that resulted from this ideological sabotage, theft, and degradation, which has continued over the centuries. I struggled with the notion that our cultural roots were being pulled up and tossed aside.

I wondered, how do we protect our heritage, simultaneously keeping it accessible to the people yet invisible from enemies, from those who would erase our history and culture to impose their own ideology?

I started to craft my response *In a Grain of Wheat*.

Just as scientists created seed banks to survive calamities of the future, I symbolically embedded a record of a lamassu (a winged lion or bull, like the one destroyed by ISIS in Nimrud) into the DNA of a grain of wheat. With a team of scientists, I translated a high-resolution 3D digital image of the human-headed winged bull of Nineveh (currently in the Metropolitan Museum of Art's collection) into a DNA sequence, and in a typical genetic engineering technique, used E. coli bacteria as a vector to inject that revised DNA into a living wheat specimen. Wheat bears deep significance for Iraq, an ancient crop domesticated by the Indigenous people of Mesopotamia and still a mainstay of the region's diet and economy. In my work, the grain of wheat also becomes a repository of historical memory, a safe haven for the image of the lamassu, so that it can be replicated and revived even if the original were to be destroyed.

This complex undertaking underscores the possibilities at the intersection of art and science. Through multidisciplinary collaboration, not only can we bridge worlds and mediate conflicts, but we can also archive material culture lost to war.

A CERTAINTY, A MIRROR, A SEED

As my life has progressed, through hardships, successes, and from project to project, I have come to believe certain things about art and what it means to be an artist.

I believe the role of the artist has shifted in recent years; we are no longer makers of objects. Rather, our purpose is to offer a platform for engagement, to spur people into action.

I believe that art, more than anything else, is the process of harvesting human connection. And to be effective, it must have clarity of purpose and it must succeed in building that genuine human connection, even in the face of injustice and oppression.

I believe that art has no singular purpose, despite our best efforts to assign one.

In fact, it is a mirror of life.

I believe that art is more about posing the right questions than offering answers, urging us all to engage the world in a meaningful way.

It can motivate us, mobilize us, inspire us.

It is feared by institutions, by society, by governments.

In this way, art remains a potent force for transformation.

For my own purposes, I've come to realize that art making was not a choice for me. My path into it was not a conscious decision but a natural progression, an organic process rooted in the details of my life.

An artist could choose to create meditative work out of personal reflection, but when fate deals one a journey like mine, that reflection becomes inherently political, and carries the responsibility and challenge of asking for engagement—and not just for awareness but participation, change.

After all, one cannot navigate an apocalypse alone, let alone survive it. You must try, in your own way, to bring people with you. For me, that has meant creating a platform for others to encounter what I've witnessed.

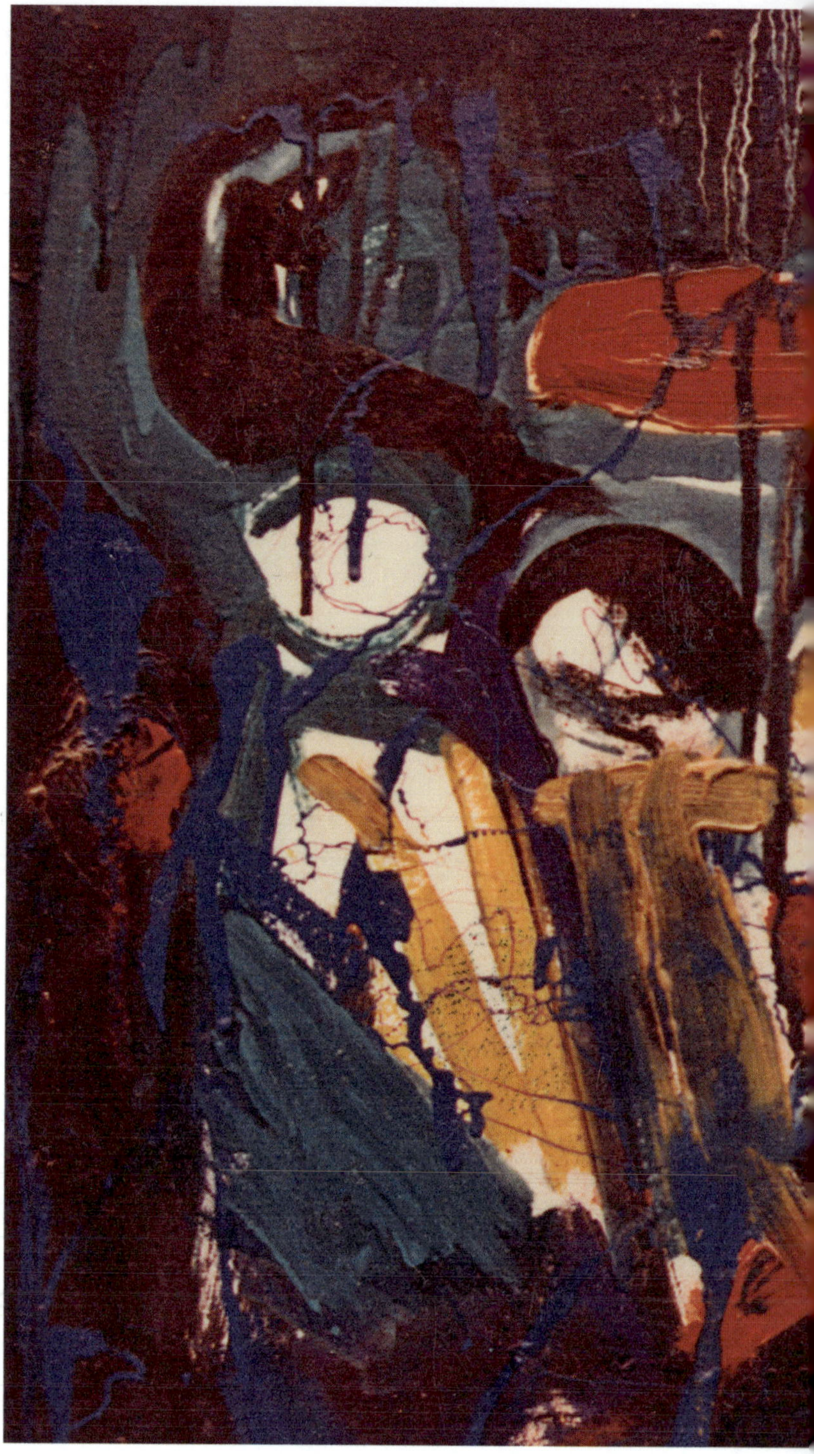

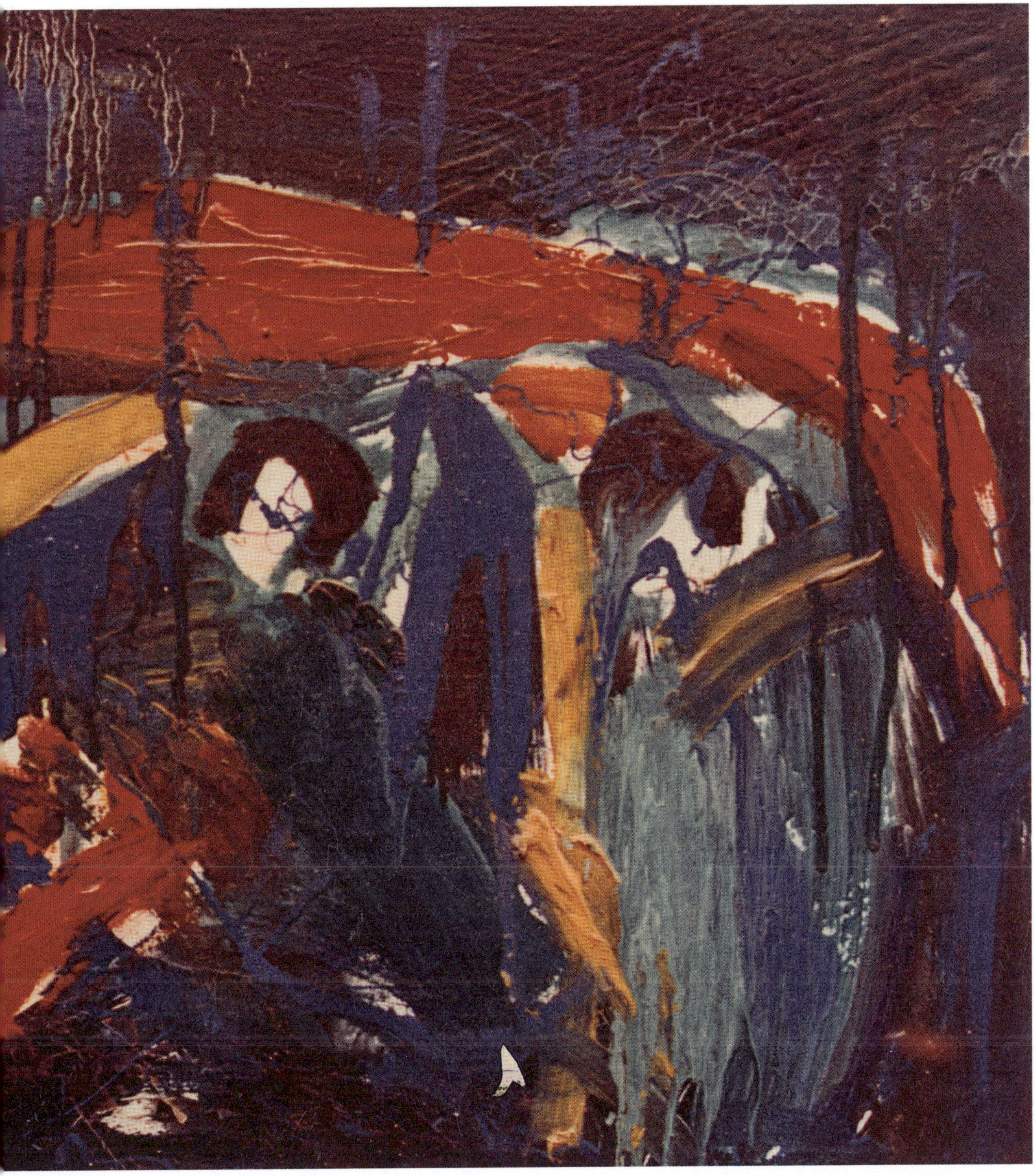

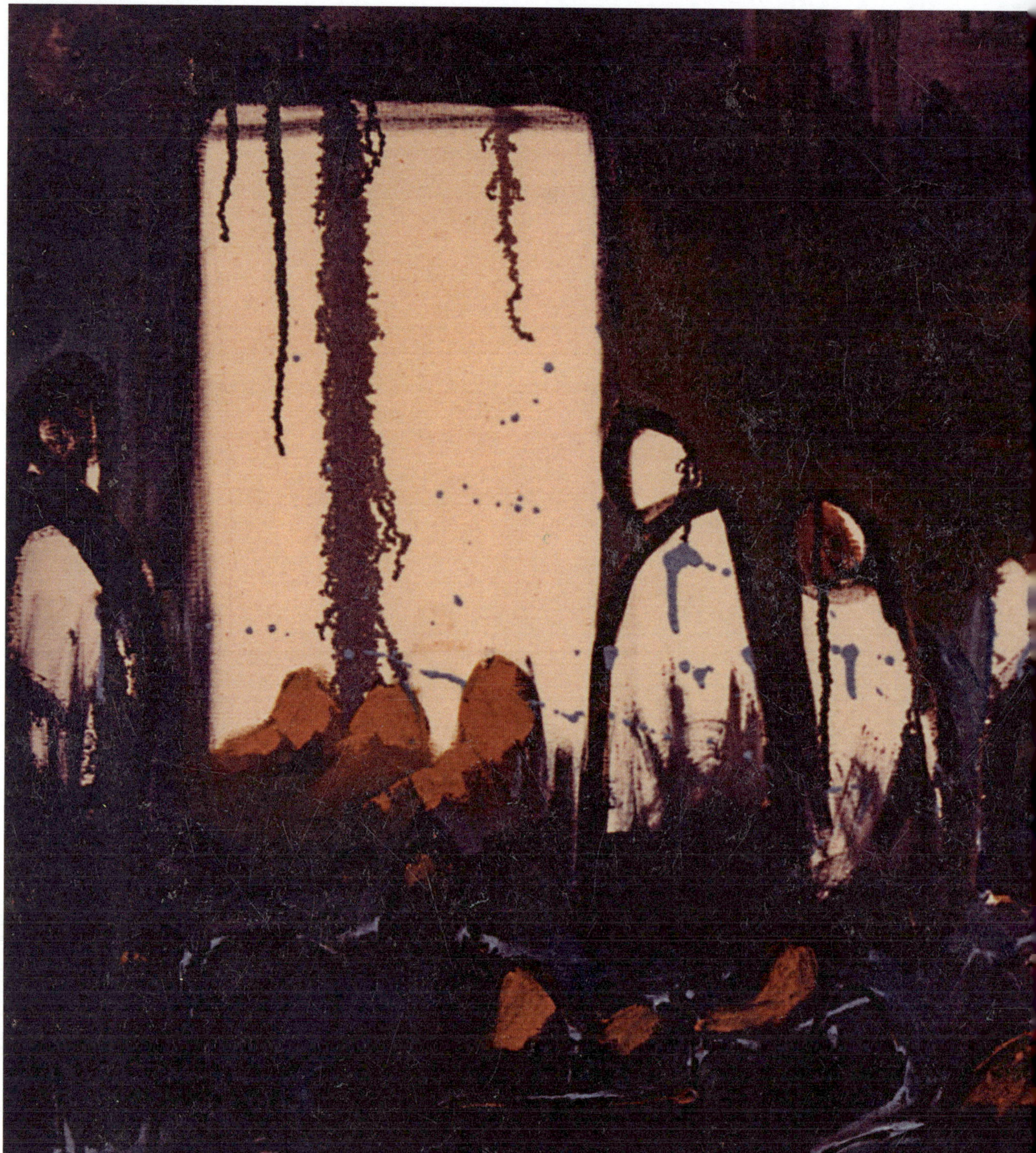

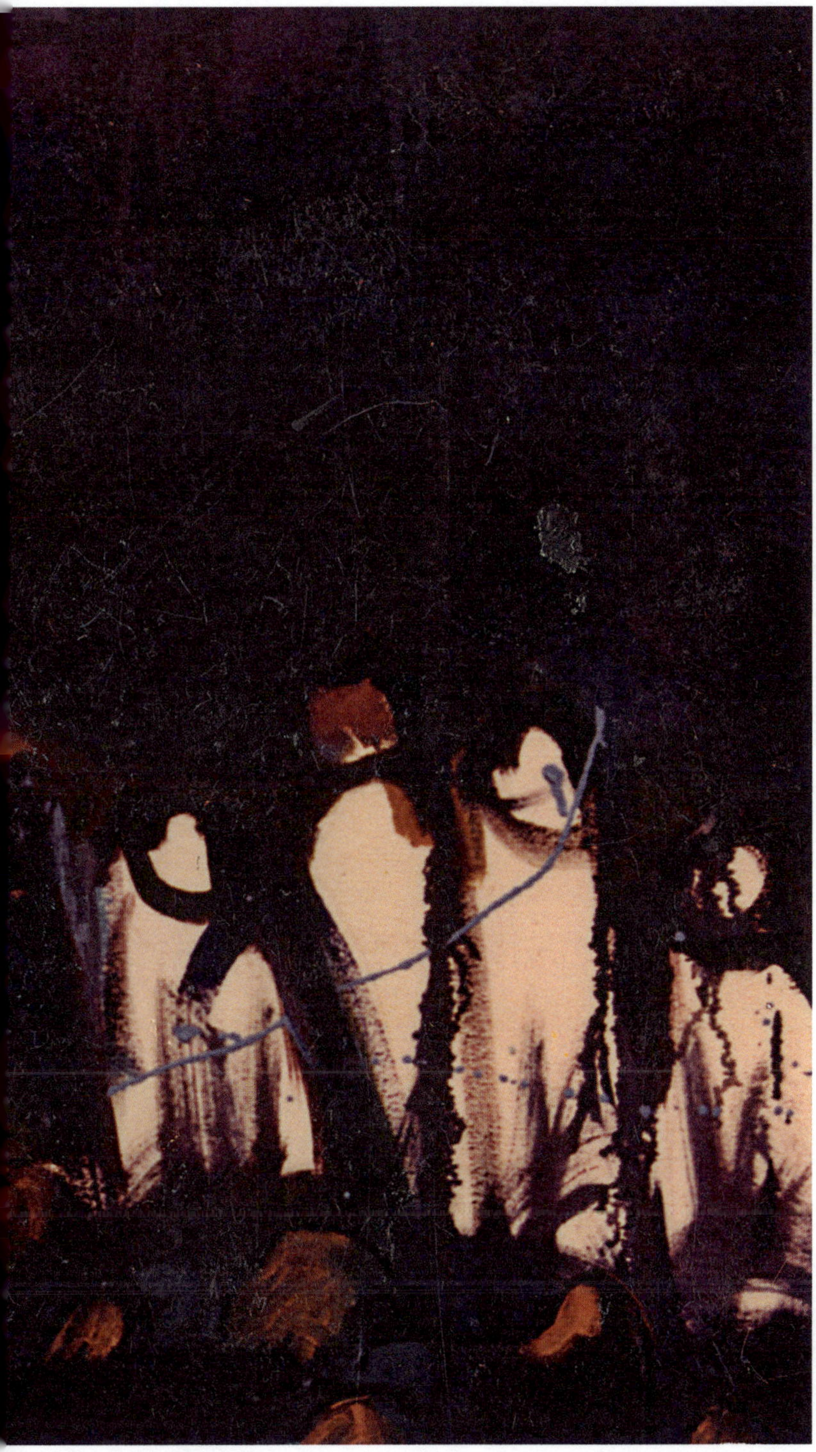

I painted these images (pp. 110–13) in the refugee camp in Saudi Arabia, using canvas ripped from the tents and a paintbrush made of my own hair. I got a job cleaning the camp early in the morning so that I could develop connections with the truck drivers delivering food and convince them to bring me art supplies. Sometimes they brought magic markers and crayons, other times the oil paint I craved. These works were created with house paint, inspired by what I experienced in the camp and by the cemetery in Najaf. They are paintings of death and destruction, with an eerie silence to them—everything melting, dripping. Painting in the camp gave me a euphoric feeling. It made me feel alive, and it gave me hope, that there was a way of getting out of the camp to continue this artistic journey.

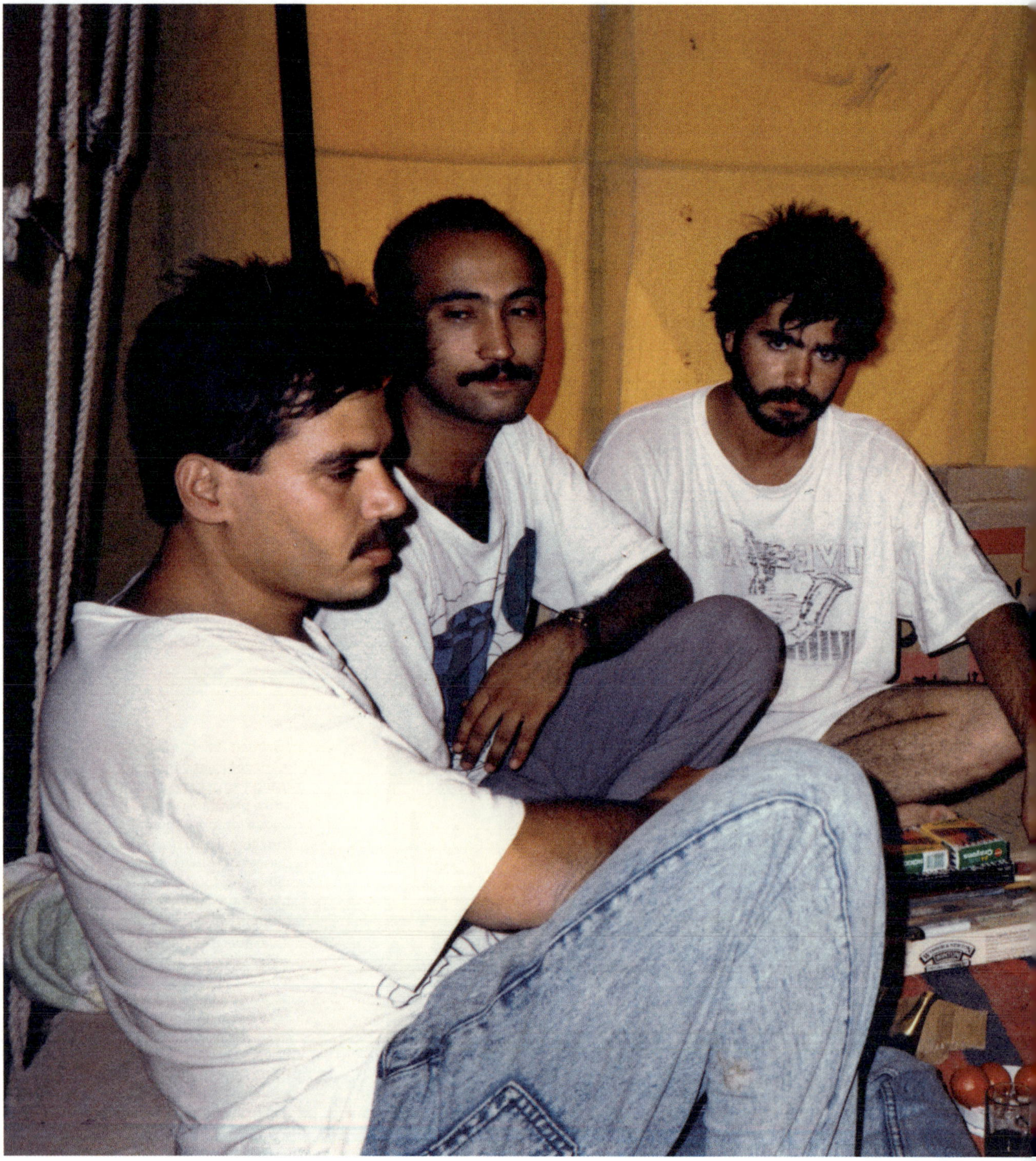

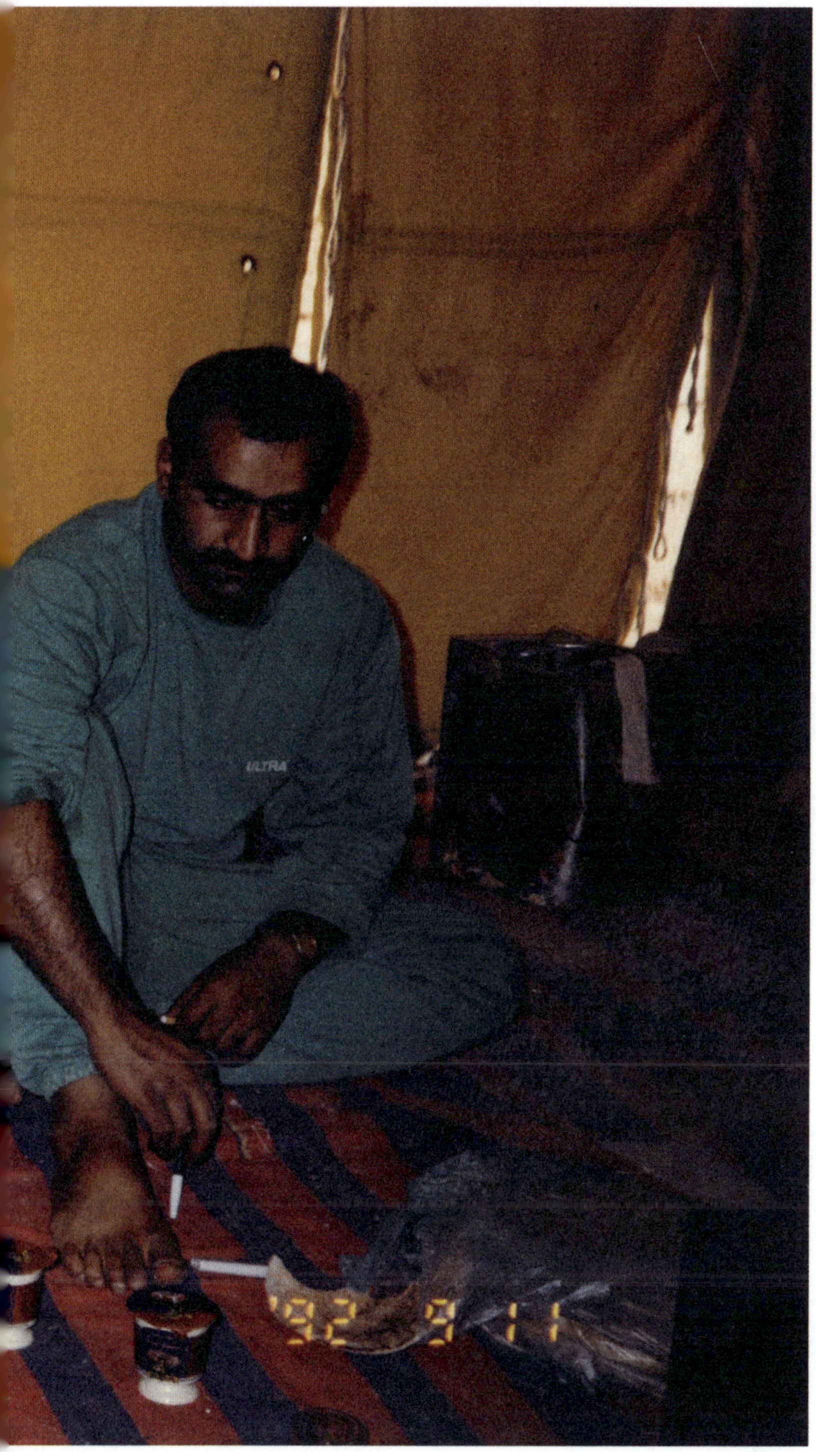

This photograph shows me (second from the right) and my brother Alaa (left), on September 11, 1992, our last night in the Rafha refugee camp in Saudi Arabia, saying goodbye to other residents. We were so cut off from outside communication, it felt like no one even knew we existed. In this image inside a tent, you can see a tin can on the lower right. I used that can as a palette for my paints. After my brother and I left, the camp remained open for years, and some people sewed their lips shut in protest, a desperate plea for help.

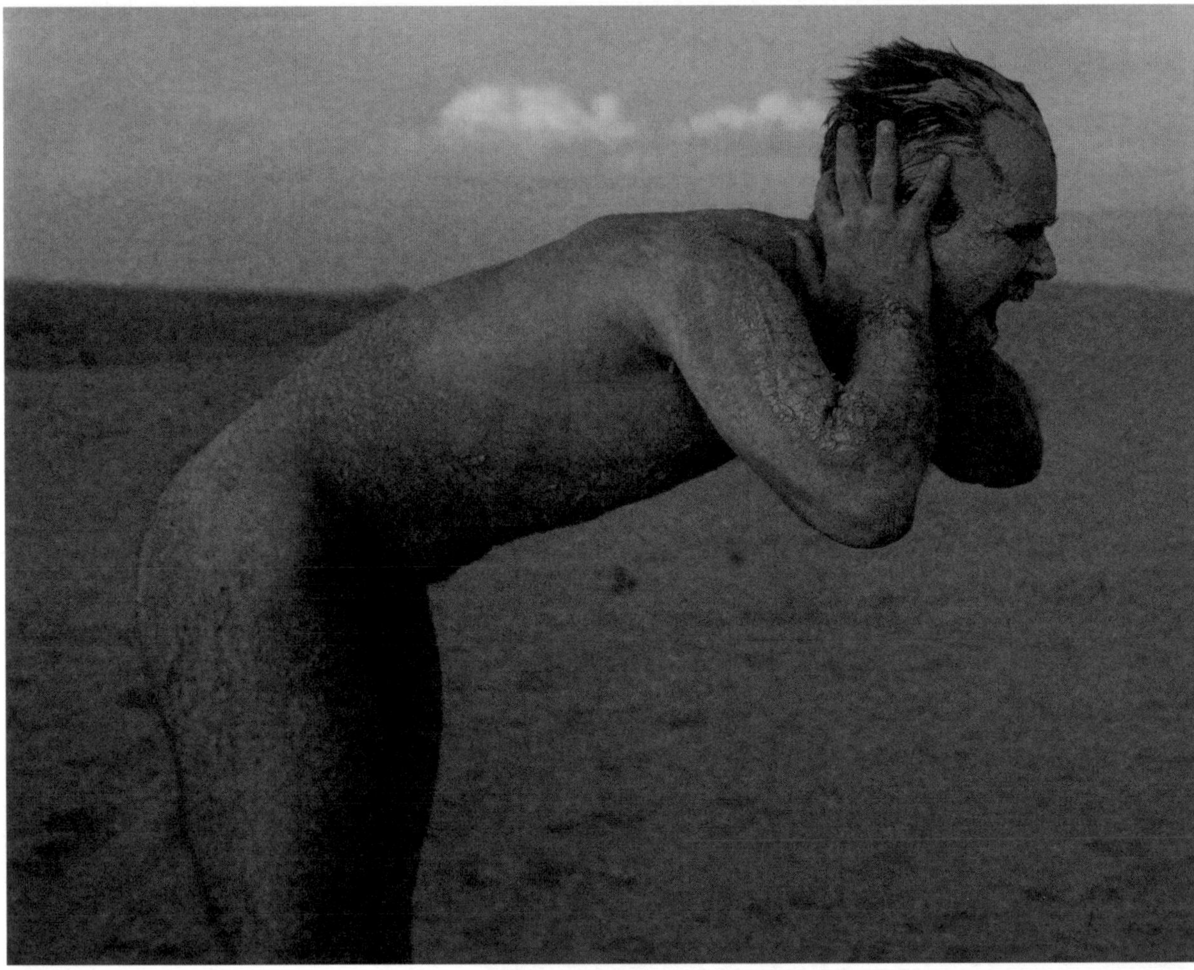

After I'd left the refugee camp and made my way to New Mexico, my friend Haydar sent me a poem he had written in the camp, titled "Ajrass," or "bells." In it, he described how we were surrounded by a cacophony of bells and chaos, and no matter how loud we screamed, no one could hear us. This was my interpretation of his poem. I covered myself in mud and buried myself up to my knees in sand, set up the speakers to represent the bells, and shot myself with a film camera. I added details to the composite image using a cutting-edge technology at the time—Photoshop. Then, I converted the image back to analog photography.

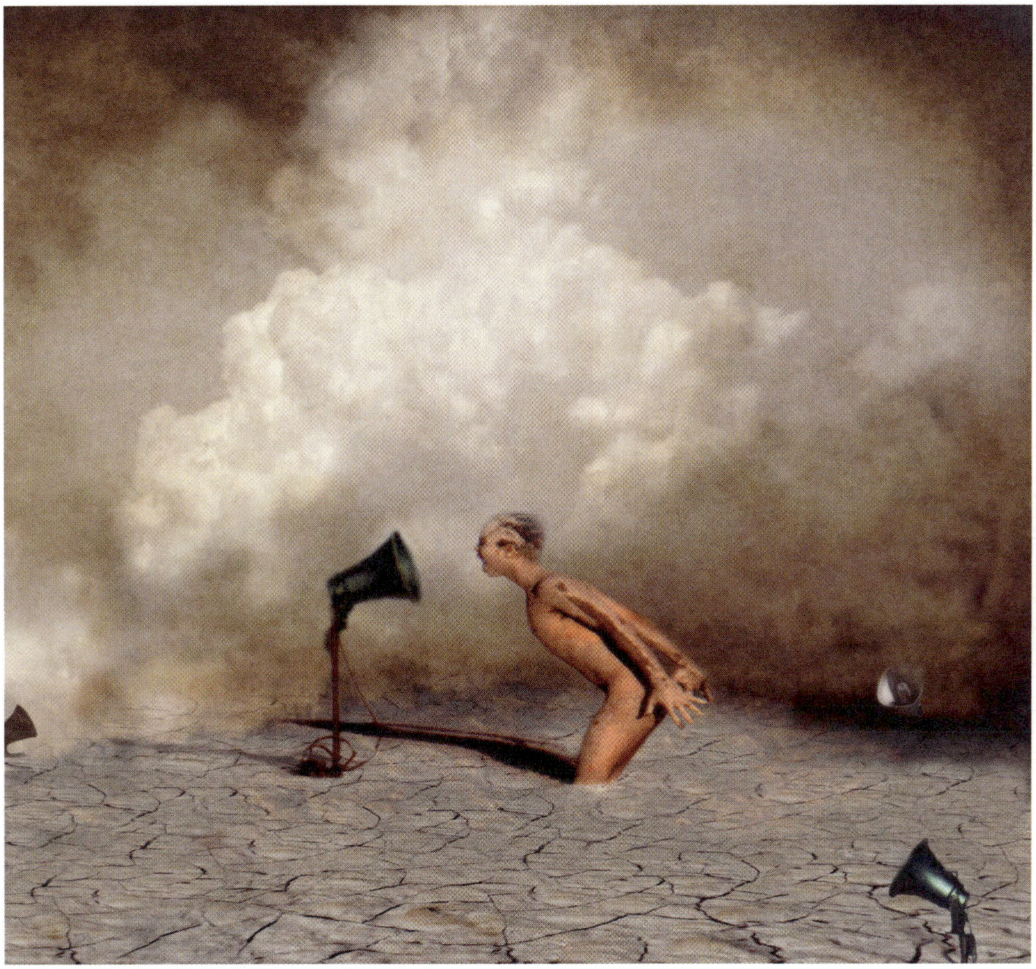

Ajrass, 1999
Digital chromogenic print
37 1/2 × 40 in. (95.3 × 101.6 cm)

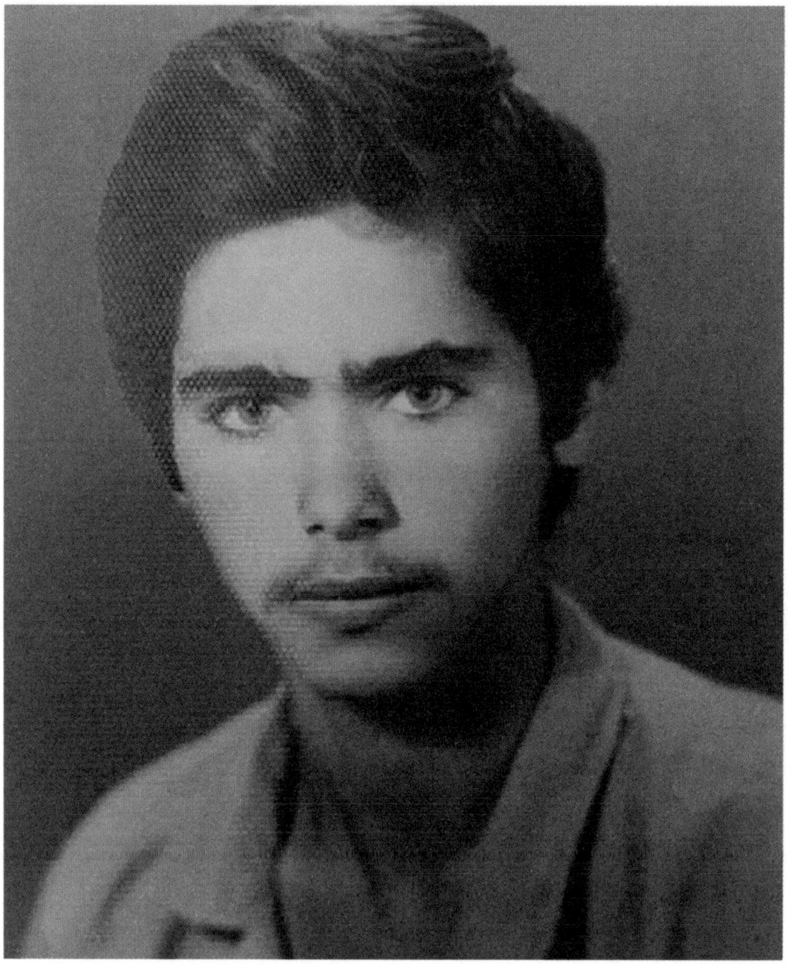

This is my school portrait from grade school in Kufa. In those years, I had a great art teacher, Hamudi. I loved studying art with him and received perfect scores. Looking at this photo, I'm reminded of the fleeting nature of calmness, peace. Soon the war with Iran started. Even at my age, we were required to participate. We trained on multiple weapons, including AK-47s. Inevitably, we lost people. We lived in this duality of life and death, where death was always on our minds. As a people, that's what made us so productive: we needed to seize every moment because we never knew when we would be gone. That's where this gaze comes from. I'm peering at life, thinking, "I want to be here, I want to be always remembered."

Born in Najaf, Iraq, in 1966
Lives and works in New York, New York

EDUCATION

2003 MFA, Art, and Technology, School of the Art Institute of Chicago, Illinois

1999 BFA, Summa Cum Laude, University of New Mexico Albuquerque

1985–90 Bachelor level coursework in Geography and Geology, University of Baghdad, Iraq

SELECTED SOLO EXHIBITIONS

2025 *Wafaa Bilal: Indulge Me*, Museum of Contemporary Art Chicago, Illinois

2022 *Gateway*, Dubai Design Week, United Arab Emirates

2021 *Wafaa Bilal: Canto III*, Natalie and James Thomson Gallery, San José State University, California

2020 *Conflict Exchange*, Chicago Cultural Center, Illinois

2016 *168:01*
Art Gallery of Windsor, Canada (2016); The Esker Foundation, Calgary, Canada (2016); Dunlop Art Gallery, Regina Public Library, Canada (2017); Arab American National Museum, Dearborn, Michigan (2017); Varley Art Gallery, Markham, Canada (2018); Confederation Centre Art Gallery, Charlottetown, Canada (2018); House of Wisdom, Sharjah, United Arab Emirates (2019)

2015 *The Things I Could Tell . . . ,* Artpace, San Antonio, Texas

Lovely Pink, Driscoll Babcock Galleries, New York, New York

I Don't Know Their Names, Linfield Gallery, Linfield College, McMinnville, Oregon

2013 *3rdi*, Doris McCarthy Gallery, University of Toronto, Scarborough, Canada

The Ashes Series
David Winton Bell Gallery, Brown University, Providence, Rhode Island (2013); Driscoll Babcock Galleries, New York, New York (2014); House of Wisdom, Sharjah, United Arab Emirates (2019)

The Hierarchy of Being, Maraya Art Park, Sharjah, United Arab Emirates

2012 *Dynamic Encounter*, Aksioma Institute for Contemporary Art, Ljubljana, Slovenia

The Comfort Zone, Lake Forest College, Lake Forest, Illinois

2010 *Wafaa Bilal*, Davidson College Art Galleries, Davidson, North Carolina

Agent Intellect, Helen Day Art Center, Stowe, Vermont

and Counting . . . , Elizabeth Foundation for the Arts, New York, New York

2008 *Virtual Jihadi*
Conference of Birds Gallery, Bangkok, Thailand (2008); Rensselaer Polytechnic Institute, Troy, New York (2008); Sanctuary for Independent Media, Troy, New York (2008)

Dog or Iraqi, Sanctuary for Independent Media, Troy, New York

2007 *Al dar Al-Iraqi* (The Iraqi House), Montalvo Arts Center, Saratoga, California

A Bar at the Folies-Bergère (after Manet), Milwaukee Art Museum, Impressionist Gallery, Wisconsin (2007); The Art Institute of Chicago, Illinois (2009)

Domestic Tension, FlatFile Gallery, Chicago, Illinois

2006 *Interior Landscapes*, Pawn Gallery, Dallas, Texas

Casting bread, Dean Jensen Gallery, Milwaukee, Wisconsin

2005 *The Human Condition*, FlatFile Gallery, Chicago, Illinois; Randy Ross Gallery, Lafayette, Indiana

2004 *Perseverance Implied*, Computing Commons Gallery, Arts, Media and Engineering, Arizona State University, Tempe

1999 *Raze #213*, ASA Gallery Albuquerque, New Mexico

Sorrow of Baghdad, Harwood Art Center, Albuquerque, New Mexico

1998 *Poliversial*, John Sommers Gallery, University of New Mexico, Albuquerque

1995 *Me-My Friends Exploring Nature*, ASA Gallery Albuquerque, New Mexico

1989 Solo exhibition, University of Baghdad, Iraq

1988 Solo exhibition, University of Baghdad, Iraq

SELECTED GROUP EXHIBITIONS

2022 *Foresight Prevents Blindness*, FNAR Gallery, University of Arkansas, Fayetteville

2020 *Art in the Age of Anxiety*, Sharjah Art Foundation, Sharjah, United Arab Emirates

2019 *Bodies of Knowledge*, New Orleans Museum of Art, Louisiana

2017 *The New Observatory*, Foundation for Art and Creative Technology, Liverpool, United Kingdom

Almost Home: Between Staying and Leaving a Phantom Land, Dorsky Gallery, New York, New York

Hello, Robot: Design Between Human and Machine, Vitra Design Museum, Weil am Rhein, Germany

The Poetics of Absence, 1X1 Gallery, Dubai, United Arab Emirates

2016 *Aspects of Gray*, Driscoll Babcock Galleries, New York, New York

Invisible Threads: Technology and Its Discontents, the Art Gallery at NYU Abu Dhabi, United Arab Emirates

Bodies in Conflict: From Gettysburg to Iraq, Schmucker Art Gallery, Gettysburg, Pennsylvania

Spheres of Influence: Codes and Conduct across Structural Landscape, Mohsen Gallery, Tehran, Iran

Contemporary Ruins: Resistance to the Spectacular Image, Wallach Art Gallery, Columbia University, New York, New York

Electronic Superhighway, Whitechapel Gallery, London, United Kingdom

The Night and the Desert Know Me, Smith Center for Healing and the Arts, Washington, DC

Polychrome, Driscoll Babcock Galleries, New York, New York

2015 The Armory Show 2015, Lawrie Shabibi Booth, New York

Crisis of History #2: Fight History, Framer Framed, Amsterdam, the Netherlands

GLOBALE: Infosphere
ZKM | Center for Art and Media Karlsruhe, Germany (2015); Centro Multimedia del Centro Nacional de las Artes, Mexico City, Mexico (2017)

Venice Biennale, Italy

Islamic Art Now: Contemporary Art of the Middle East, Los Angeles County Museum of Art, California

2014 *A Room of His Own: Masculinities in Korea and the Middle East*, Art Sonje Center, Seoul, Korea

Daegu International Multimedia Art Festival, Daegu, Korea

Dead Serious, 47 Internationale Ferienkurse Für Neue Musik, Darmstadt, Germany

The Other and Me, Sharjah Art Museum, Sharjah, United Arab Emirates

Multiple Exposures: Jewelry and Photography, Museum of Arts and Design, New York, New York

Art Dubai, Dubai, United Arab Emirates

2013 *MENA Viceroy: Exploring Identity and Conflict in a Post-Colonial World*, Levantine Cultural Center, Los Angeles, California

An I for an Eye, Austrian Cultural Forum New York, New York

Contained Conflict, Driscoll Babcock Gallery, New York, New York

Annual Rapid Pulse International Performance Art Festival, Chicago, Illinois

Art Dubai, Dubai, United Arab Emirates

The Public Private, Anna-Maria and Stephen Kellen Gallery, Parsons School of Design, New York, New York

2012 Impakt, *No More Westerns*, Utrecht, the Netherlands

Abandon Normal Devices, Manchester, United Kingdom

Subversion of Comedies, Cornerhouse, Manchester, United Kingdom

Voyeur, Truman State University Art Gallery, Kirksville, Missouri

2011 The Jakarta Biennale #14, *Jakarta Maximum City: Survive or Escape*, Jakarta, Indonesia

What Matters Now: Proposals for a New Front Page, Aperture Foundation, New York, New York

Christie's Dubai Auction Benefitting Echo for Contemporary Iraqi Art, Dubai, United Arab Emirates

Requiem for Innocence, Aaran Art Gallery, Tehran, Iran

A Call, White Box, New York, New York

Out of Rubble
SPACE Gallery, Pittsburgh, Pennsylvania (2011); Dorothy Uber Bryan Gallery, Bowling Green State University, Bowling Green, Ohio (2012); The Marlin and Regina Miller Gallery, Kutztown State University, Kutztown, Pennsylvania (2012); String Room Gallery, Wells College, Aurora, New York (2013); Harris Art Gallery, University of La Verne, La Verne, California (2013); Schmucker Art Gallery at Gettysburg College, Gettysburg, Pennsylvania (2014); Jack Olsen Gallery at Northern Illinois University, Dekalb (2014); Center of Art, Design, and Visual Culture, University of Maryland, Baltimore (2015)

2011 *Blown Up: Gaming and War*
InterAccess Electronic Media Arts Center, Toronto, Canada (2011); MAI, Montreal, Canada (2012); Gallery 101 Ottawa, Canada (2013); Latitude 53 Gallery, Alberta, Canada (2014)

Looking Back, Moving Forward, Richard F. Brush Gallery, St. Lawrence University, New York, New York

ASPECT: The Chronicle of New Media Art, Volume 14: Middle East, Yerba Buena Center for the Arts, San Francisco, California

Regard, Resist, React, Governors State University Visual Arts Gallery, Parkway, Illinois

Serious Games, Mathildenhöhe Darmstadt, Darmstadt, Germany

The Relentless Eye: Global Cell Phone Photography, Marshall Fine Arts Center, Haverford, Pennsylvania

2010 *Told, Untold, Retold*, Mathaf: Arab Museum of Modern Art, Doha, Qatar

TIME AFTER TIME: ACTIONS AND INTERACTIONS, Southern Exposure, San Francisco, California

The Interrupted Image, Nicholas Robinson Gallery, New York

The Technology Show, Gallatin Galleries, New York University, New York

The Armory Show, New York, New York

2009 *America*, Beirut Art Center, Lebanon

Forbidden Junctions, Israeli Art Center for Visual Art, Holon, Israel

Its Darkest Places: War Illuminated, Powerhouse Arena, Brooklyn, New York

L'École du Magasin, Season 18, Centre National d'Art Contemporain de Grenoble, Grenoble, France

Techno_Culture, Redhouse Arts Center, Syracuse, New York

2191 Days and Counting . . . , Powerhouse, Brooklyn, New York

2008 *Experiencing the War in Iraq*, Pawtucket Armory, Providence, Rhode Island

Sedition, White Box, New York, New York

Site Unseen, Chicago Cultural Center, Illinois

Virtual Jihadi
FlatFile Gallery, Chicago, Illinois (2008); *Welcome to the Terrordome*, Museum of Contemporary Canadian Art, Toronto, Canada (2009); Spark Festival, University of Minnesota, Minneapolis (2009); Syracuse University, New York (2009); Dowd Gallery, State University of New York, Cortland (2009); Centre National d'Art Contemporain de Grenoble, Grenoble, France (2009); Kleefeld Gallery, Hamburg, Germany (2009); Beirut Art Center, Lebanon (2010)

2007 *Consuming War*, Hyde Park Art Center, Chicago, Illinois

Bilingual: Art at the Intersection of Painting and Video, Glass Curtain Gallery, Columbia College, Chicago, Illinois

This Is Not A Self-Portrait, Gallery 2, School of the Art Institute of Chicago, Illinois

Global Eyes, ACM Siggraph 2007 Art Gallery, San Diego, California

To Fear or Not to Fear, The Art Center of Highland Park, Highland Park, Illinois

2006 *Imagine: Hope, Peace, and Justice*, Tippecanoe Arts Federation, Lafayette, Indiana

ACTIVE LIBERTY, School of the Art Institute of Chicago, Illinois

DETAINED, Asian American Arts Centre, New York, New York

2005 *Footcandles: History and Process in Contemporary Photography*, Indiana State University, The University Art Gallery, Bloomington

The Institute Show, Albany Institute of History and Art, Albany, New York

Cyclics Art Show, Cyclics Corporation, Schenectady, New York

Midwest Olympia, The Museum of Contemporary Photography, Chicago, Illinois

2004 *Intimachine*, Art Interactive Gallery Cambridge, Massachusetts

GLOBAL Vision 2003, FlatFile Gallery, Chicago, Illinois

Thesis Exhibition, Gallery 2, School of the Art Institute of Chicago, Illinois

2002 *Al Qaeda R Us*
Gallery 2, School of the Art Institute of Chicago, Illinois (2002); G2 Immersion, Point Lipa Gallery, Chicago, Illinois (2004); Green Zone, Red Zone, Gemeentemuseum Den Haag, Netherlands (2007)

2001 *Security System*, site-specific performance and installation, Chicago, Illinois

1997 *Prints*, Gyros Gallery, Albuquerque, New Mexico

Enduring Look, 1926 Exhibition Studies Space, Chicago, Illinois

2023 Pizarro, Citlali. "Serious Play: The Art of Wafaa Bilal and Tasneem Mandviwala." *American Theater*, November 14, 2023.

2021 Čvoro, Uroš, and Kit Messham-Muir. *Images of War in Contemporary Art: Terror and Conflict in the Mass Media*. New York: Bloomsbury, 2021.

Rosier, Howard J. "Wafaa Bilal Explores the Power of Technology." *School of the Art Institute of Chicago* magazine, Fall 2021.

Stone, Mina. "Cooking with Artists: Wafaa Bilal." *MoMA Magazine*, July 13, 2021.

2020 "2021 Creative Capital Award Recipients Announced," *Artforum*, December 8, 2020.

Dixon, Steve. *Cybernetic-Existentialism: Freedom, Systems, and Being-for-Others in Contemporary Arts and Performance*. New York: Routledge, 2020.

2019 Ditmars, Hadani. "Veterans and Artists Draw Creative Profit Out of War," *The Art Newspaper*, May 7, 2019.

Schriwer, Charlotte, and Nele Lenze, eds. *Participation Culture in the Gulf: Networks, Politics and Identity*. New York: Routledge, 2019.

2018 Bilal, Wafaa. "The Ashes Series." *Public* 29, no. 58 (2018): 79–83.

Vaughan, R. M. "Critics' Pick: Wafaa Bilal, Aga Khan Museum." *Artforum*, 2018.

2017 Feldman, Zeena, ed. *Art and the Politics of Visibility: Contesting the Global, Local and the In-Between*. New York: Bloomsbury, 2017.

Kattan, Bana, and Scott Fitzgerald. *Invisible Threads: Technology and its Discontents*, NYU Abu Dhabi Art Gallery.

Paulsen, Kris. "The View from Here: Remote Action and the Trauma of (Not) Being Touched." In *Here/There: Telepresence, Touch, and Art at the Interface*. Cambridge, MA: MIT Press, 2017.

2016 Aima, Rahel. "Against the Widening Gulf: Arab Art in Tehran." *Art in America*, May 6, 2016.

Bausells, Marta. "Artist's 'Blank Books' Project Seeks to Restock Historic Baghdad Library." *Guardian*, January 26, 2016.

Kapadia, Ronak K. "Up in the Air and on the Skin: Drone Warfare and the Queer Calculus of Pain." In *Critical Ethnic Studies: A Reader*, edited by Nada Elia et al. Durham, NC: Duke University Press, 2016.

Mitra, Srimoyee, ed. *Wafaa Bilal: 168:01*. Art Gallery of Windsor and Esker Foundation, 2016.

Morrison, Elise. *Discipline and Desire: Surveillance Technologies in Performance*. Ann Arbor: University of Michigan Press, 2016.

2015 Bilal, Wafaa. "Erasing." *Ibraaz*. October 29, 2015.

Mamou, Regina. "Islamic Art Now: A Conversation with Wafaa Bilal." *Art Muse*.

Unger, Clio. "'SHOOT HIM NOW!!!' Anonymity, Accountability and Online Spectatorship in Wafaa Bilal's *Domestic Tension*." *International Journal of Performance and Digital Media* 11, no. 2 (2015): 202–218.

2014 Bilal, Wafaa. "Dynamic Encounters and the Benjaminian Aura." In *The Routledge Companion to Art and Politics*, edited by Randy Martin. New York: Routledge, 2014.

Bilal, Wafaa, and Shelley Rice. *Wafaa Bilal: The Ashes Series*. Driscoll Babcock Galleries, 2014.

Jablon, Samuel. "Wafaa Bilal's War of Images." *Hyperallergic*, July 10, 2014.

Krule, Jackson. "Wafaa Bilal's 'The Ashes Series.'" *New Yorker*, May 28, 2014.

2013 Al-Ali, Nadje, and Deborah Al-Najjar, eds. *We are Iraqis: Aesthetics and Politics in a Time of War*. Syracuse, NY: Syracuse University Press, 2013.

Anderson, Kurt. "About Face." *PRI's The World*, August 15, 2013.

Raza, Sara. "Wafaa Bilal: After the Dust Settles." *Canvas* 9, no. 5 (September 2013).

2012

Rice, Shelley. "Domestic Tension: An Interview with Wafaa Bilal." *Le Magazine Jeu de Paume Paris*, October 1, 2012.

2011

Rawlings, Ashley. "Wafaa Bilal: Remote Repercussions." *Art Asia Pacific* 72 (March/April 2011): 84–93.

Rymer, Michael. "Skull Captures: An NYU Photography Professor Prepares to Reinstall a Webcam in the Back of His Head." *Village Voice*, August 10, 2011.

Slavick, Susanne, ed. *Out of Rubble*. Milan, Italy: Charta, 2011.

Taylor, Kate. "No More Looking Backward: Professor Has Camera Removed From His Head." *New York Times*, February 10, 2011.

2010

Adeeb, Ali. "105,000 Dots for Iraq, and Counting." *City Room Blog, New York Times*, March 4, 2010.

Goodman, Amy. "105,000 Tattoos: Iraqi Artist Wafaa Bilal Turns His Own Body into a Canvas to Commemorate Dead Iraqis and Americans." *Democracy Now!*, March 9, 2010.

Keefe, Alexander. "Critics' Pick: Wafaa Bilal, Helen Day Art Center." *Artforum*, 2010.

Orden, Erica. "His Hindsight Is 20-20: In First Interview, NYU Professor Is 'Uncomfortable for Sure.'" *Wall Street Journal*, December 3, 2010.

2009

ASPECT: The Chronicle of New Media Art 14: Middle East, Fall 2009.

"Domestic Tension: Art Under a Gun." Colors 75, April 1, 2009.

Guez, Dor. *Forbidden Junctions*. The Israeli Center for Digital Art, 2009.

Johnson, Bobbie. "US Campaigners File Lawsuit Over George Bush Assassination Game." *Guardian*, June 12, 2009.

Lamendola, Michael. "Civil Liberties Union Sues Troy for Shutting Down Arts Facility." *Daily Gazette*, June 9, 2009.

Losh, Elizabeth. *Virtualpolitik: An Electronic History of Government Media-Making in a Time of War, Scandal, Disaster, Miscommunication, and Mistakes*. Cambridge, MA: MIT Press, 2009.

2008

Bilal, Wafaa, and Kari Lydersen. *Shoot an Iraqi: Art, Life, and Resistance Under the Gun*. San Francisco, CA: City Lights Books, 2009.

Franco, James. "NYCLU Sues Troy Over Controversial Exhibit." *Troy Record*, June 10, 2008.

Lamendola, Michael. "Sanctuary Displaying 'Virtual Jihadi' Closed." *Daily Gazette*, March 12, 2008.

Shulman, Robin. "Terror-Themed Game Suspended Iraqi-Born Artist Asserts Censorship After Exhibit Is Shut Down." *Washington Post*, March 8, 2008.

Werman, Marco. "Shoot an Iraqi?" *PRI's The World*, December 18, 2008.

2007

Artner, Alan G. "Wafaa Bilal: Interactive Performance Piece Is Altering Perspectives on War, One Paintball at a Time." *Chicago Tribune*, December 30, 2007.

Caro, Mark, "A Point-and-Shoot Exhibit." *Chicago Tribune*, May 10, 2007.

Lawson, Sean, and Wafaa Bilal. "A Look at Crudeoils." *Media in Transition 5: Creativity, Ownership and Collaboration in the Digital Age*, April 27, 2007.

Lydersen, Kari. "Antiwar Art in a New Medium: Paintball-on-Web." *Washington Post*, May 29, 2007.

2002

Sarlin, Paige. "Addressing the World from the Midwest: An Interview with Iraqi-born Artist Wafaa Bilal." *F Newsmagazine*, December 2002.

EXHIBITION CHECKLIST

Descriptions for how artworks were presented for *Wafaa Bilal: Indulge Me* at the Museum of Contemporary Art Chicago (February 1–October 19, 2025) are included below the relevant captions.

Domestic Tension, 2007
Durational performance
Courtesy of the artist
MCA presentation: Archival performance ephemera installed in a replica of the room in which the 2007 performance at FlatFile Gallery, Chicago, took place.

Virtual Jihadi, 2008
Video game
Courtesy of the artist
MCA presentation: A playable version of *Virtual Jihadi* hosted at three computer stations installed in a replica of an internet café.

3rdi, 2010–11
Durational performance
Mathaf: Arab Museum of Modern Art, Doha, Qatar
MCA presentation: A 14-foot screen displaying minute-by-minute images from the *3rdi* performance, synchronized to the date and time they were originally captured.

Canto III, 2015
Bronze with gold finish
37 × 26 3/4 × 15 in. (94 × 67.9 × 38.1 cm)
Courtesy of the artist

Rendering of Canto III, 2023
Vinyl
25.6 × 20 ft. (7.8 × 6.1 m)
Courtesy of the artist

Thumbsat Model, 2024
Selfie micro camera, transmitter, battery, GPS, vane, shape-memory alloy tail/antenna, and 3D-printed, 21 carat gold-plated bust
Two parts, each: 16 × 10 × 10 in. (40.6 × 25.4 × 25.4 cm)
Editions 1 and 2 of 3
Courtesy of the artist
MCA presentation: Edition 1 of *Thumbsat Model* planned for launch into lower Earth orbit; Edition 2 displayed in gallery alongside a "ground station" comprising a computer, a radio, a desk, and a video projector displaying live tracking of Edition 1 in space.

Lamassu (In a Grain of Wheat), 2025
High-resolution 3D print and bioengineered wheat grains containing a 3D scan of a lamassu within its DNA
84 × 84 × 30 in. (213.4 × 213.4 × 76.2 cm)
Commissioned by the Museum of Contemporary Art Chicago

LENDERS

Wafaa Bilal
Mathaf: Arab Museum of Modern Art, Qatar

SPONSORS

Lead support is provided by the Harris Family Foundation in memory of Bette and Neison Harris, the Zell Family Foundation, and Cari and Michael Sacks.

Generous support is provided by Creative Capital Foundation, The Joyce Foundation, and the Margot and W. George Greig Ascendant Artist Fund.

Creative Capital | The Joyce Foundation

BANA KATTAN
Bana Kattan, Pamela Alper Associate Curator, MCA Chicago, is a researcher and curator with experience working in the Arab world and the United States. Prior to her time at the MCA, she was the Curator at the New York University Abu Dhabi Art Gallery and researcher for Arab Art Historian Salwa Mikdadi. She received her MA from the School of the Art Institute of Chicago in 2011 and is a recipient of the Barjeel Global Fellowship (2018–19) and a CAA-Getty International Program Grant (2015).

LYNN HERSHMAN LEESON
Artist and filmmaker Lynn Hershman Leeson is widely recognized for her innovative work investigating issues including the relationship between humans and technology; identity; surveillance; and the use of media as a tool of empowerment against censorship and political repression. Her six feature films—*The Electronic Diaries* (1984–96), *Conceiving Ada* (1997), *Teknolust* (2002), *Strange Culture* (2007), *!Women Art Revolution: A Secret History* (2010), *Tania Libre* (2016)—are in worldwide distribution. She is a recipient of awards including a Siggraph Lifetime Achievement Award, Prix Ars Electronica Golden Nica, and a John Simon Guggenheim Memorial Foundation Fellowship. In 2022, she was awarded a special mention from the jury for her participation in the 59th Venice Biennale. In 2023, the Pratt Institute in Brooklyn, New York, awarded her with an honorary doctorate. In 2023, she received a Distinguished Artist Award from Creative Capital. Hershman Leeson's artwork is featured in many public collections, including the Museum of Modern Art and the San Francisco Museum of Modern Art, which acquired its first NFT from Hershman Leeson in 2023.

WAFAA BILAL
Iraqi-born artist Wafaa Bilal is known internationally for his online, performative, and interactive works provoking dialogue about international and interpersonal politics. Bilal's work explores tensions between the cultural spaces he occupies—his home in the comfort zone of the United States and his consciousness in the "conflict zone" in Iraq. In 2008, the *Chicago Tribune* named him Artist of the Year. That same year, City Lights published *Shoot an Iraqi: Art, Life and Resistance Under the Gun*, a book about Bilal's life and *Domestic Tension*. His artwork is featured in the permanent collections of the Los Angeles County Museum of Art, California; the Museum of Contemporary Photography, Chicago, Illinois; and Mathaf: Arab Museum of Modern Art, Doha, Qatar; among others. He holds a BFA from the University of New Mexico, an MFA from the School of the Art Institute of Chicago, and was conferred an honorary doctorate from DePauw University. Bilal is currently an Arts Professor at NYU's Tisch School of the Arts.

Cover and back cover, p. 82 (detail): *Rendering of Thumbsat Model*, 2024. Photo: Omar ElGamal.

Title page: Portrait of Wafaa Bilal during his 2007 performance, *Domestic Tension*. Photo: Kirk Gittings.

Detail, pp. 12, 92–3: Sketch of the MCA-commissioned *Lamassu (In a Grain of Wheat)* sculpture. Illustration: James Kloiber.

Detail, p. 30: Gun maintenance sign used by Wafaa Bilal during his 2007 performance, *Domestic Tension*. Photo: James Kloiber.

Detail, p. 96: Sketch of the *3rdi* camera apparatus and installation plan. Illustration: Kevin McElroy.

REPRODUCTION CREDITS

Credits are listed by page number. Every reasonable attempt has been made to locate the owners of copyrights and to ensure the credit information supplied is accurately listed. Errors or omissions will be corrected in future editions.

Unless otherwise noted, all artworks are reproduced courtesy of the artist. The following applies to images for which additional acknowledgment is due:

20: Photo: Stuart Franklin/Magnum;
21: CPA Media Pte Ltd/Alamy Stock Photo;
25: Michael Gonzalez/Getty Images;
34, 41, 43: © Lynn Hershman Leeson;
34: Photo: Franz Wamhof;
41: Photo: Tobias Wootton;
43: Photo: Tate;
47: Photo: Brad Farwell;
52 (top): Website reconstruction: Rhizome;
60–1: Illustration: James Kloiber;
64–5: Photo: Ben Pier, Art Asia Pacific 72 (March/April 2011);
66: Illustrations: Kevin McElroy;
77, 87, 90: Photos: Dhemerae K Ford;
84–5: Video stills © MCA Chicago;
86: Photo: Shawn Larson, 2024.

FAIR USE STATEMENT

The MCA asserts its Fair Use rights in the reproduction of comparative illustrations in its exhibition catalogues. Essays, timelines, interviews, and other scholarly texts are often accompanied by images to help clarify concepts and enhance readers' overall understanding of the subject matter. According to the Association of Art Museum Directors' Guidelines for the Use of Copyrighted Materials and Works of Art by Art Museums, these uses should be "confined, In the extent of copyrighted materials and in the size and quality of images of works of art, to that necessary to illustrate the educational, scholarly or critical text and no more." We adhere to these standards and make every reasonable attempt to ensure the accuracy of credit and caption information for each image. We welcome any uncredited creators to come forward so that we may acknowledge them and correct any errors or omissions in future editions.

This book is published on the occasion of the exhibition *Wafaa Bilal: Indulge Me*, organized by the Museum of Contemporary Art Chicago, curated by Bana Kattan, Pamela Alper Associate Curator, with Iris Colburn, Curatorial Associate, and presented in the Bergman Family Gallery at the Museum of Contemporary Art Chicago, February 1–October 19, 2025.

View the exhibition video and installation shots online at https://visit.mcachicago.org/exhibitions/wafaa-bilal-indulge-me/.

Published as part of the *Ascendant Artist* series by the Museum of Contemporary Art Chicago and DelMonico Books • D.A.P.

MCA CHICAGO

Museum of Contemporary Art Chicago
220 E Chicago Ave
Chicago, IL 60611
312-280-2660

DelMonico Books
Available through ARTBOOK | D.A.P.
75 Broad Street, Suite 630
New York, NY 10004
artbook.com
delmonicobooks.com

For Museum of Contemporary Art Chicago
Director of Content Strategy:
Kelsey Campbell-Dollaghan
Associate Director of Editorial: Tyler Laminack
Associate Director of Rights and Images:
Katie Levi
Rights and Images Coordinator:
Gabrielle Banks
Content Strategy Intern: Marcelo Quesada
Content Strategy Intern: Ricky Reyes

Copyeditor: Matthew Christensen

For their support on his essay, Wafaa Bilal would like to thank Kari Lydersen and Rah Eleh.

Designed by: Larry Issa

Printed and bound in Slovakia.

Library of Congress Control Number: 2024946835

ISBN: 978-1-63681-157-4

05/20/07
24.201.201.241: the problem is you think one man leads us to war
72.66.79.84: http://wafaabilal.com//chat/simplechat.php
24.201.201.241: we led ourselves to war
69.3.220.149: there was a lot of confusion around the election
24.19.97.242: oh christ
69.3.220.149: 241, that is a good point
69.3.220.149: but i'm not sure how i was responsible for that
69.3.220.149: but i think that osama wants me dead

05/20/07
24.201.201.241: we know whats right/wrong
24.201.201.241: listen. dont believe anything
24.201.201.241: learn
69.3.220.149: listen to people, and then decide what is right
72.66.79.84: Yeah, fuck the politics, just shoot Wafaa

05/20/07
72.66.79.84: he's practically asking for it.
69.3.220.149: he didn't put himself in that position
72.66.79.84: yes he did
69.3.220.149: he's demonstrating a position that already exists
69.3.220.149: iraqis didn't put themselves in that position
91.152.239.48: I chose not to pull the trigger.

05/20/07
72.66.79.84: choosing to hit the trigger is fun
71.87.43.86: .84, may I ask why?
69.3.220.149: fun is not always the point
69.3.220.149: there are more important things than fun

05/20/07
207.229.189.214: when is the gun going to be pointed at us?

05/20/07
71.87.43.86: I wish one of the options was a cease fire

05/20/07
68.51.193.138: People what are you thinking about this project?
72.178.49.71: i think it's interesting, but people are people...
69.3.220.149: i like this project
72.178.49.71: and it is difficult to change people's mind
69.3.220.149: i've learned that too, 71.